Keep believing
for a miracle!
Mark 9:23
Holly Murray

Family photo on back cover courtesy of Haley Lamb.

Believing for a Miracle

Our Journey of Faith, Miracles, and the Healing of Cancer

HOLLY MURRAY

Dedication

I dedicate this book to my family who walked every step of this journey with me.

To my husband Keith, you are my rock and biggest cheerleader. You kept calling me author before I believed I could even do it. To my son Caleb - Baby, this is your story of what God did in our lives. You have strength like no one I know, and you will always be my favorite bassist. To my son Joshua, you make me laugh when I feel like crying and the way you love and share Jesus with others is inspiring to me. You have more compassion in you than anyone I know, and your skills on the drums are mind boggling to me! I know God has some mighty big things ahead for us all, and I can hardly wait to find out what they are.

For I know the plans I have for you," says the LORD.
"They are plans for good and not for disaster,
to give you a future and a hope."
Jeremiah 29:11

A Note from the Author

Dear Reader,

Everyone has a story and every story is different. Every story has divine purpose which can alter the life of someone who hears it. Finally, every story is unending as long as it can be told and remembered. This story is mine. I pray that as you read it you will find great encouragement to face and conquer your own battles, and to find the strength to share your own story with others. That is one way you can make a tremendous impact on the world for the kingdom of God. I also pray that if you have never asked Jesus to be your personal Savior, that you will ask Him into your heart as you read this book. He loves you so much, and there is no greater joy and peace than living life with Him as Lord and center of it all.

Declare His glory among the nations,
His wonderful works among all peoples.
Psalm 96:3 (HCSB)

Acknowledgements

Thank you, to my heavenly Father, for gifting me with this life, salvation, and the strength to share my story with others.

Thank you, Keith, for loving me. Thank you for always supporting my ideas and making me believe in myself. You've been doing that for 27 years and counting. To my boys, Caleb and Joshua, thank you both for making me a mama and keeping me on my toes since before each of you were born. I have learned more about my Father because of you two.

To my mom and dad, Allan and Frankye Wasson, I am who I am because of the training and foundation you laid for me. Dad, you taught me how to be a daughter to the King by being an example of a good father. I have never been afraid of God. Mom, you taught me how to be a wife and a mom, and those are my highest callings in life.

To my in-laws, Carroll and Brenda Binns, I love you like I was your daughter because that is how you have always treated me. I am so thankful that I am a part of your crazy fun family.

To my siblings, siblings-in-law, their spouses, and my nieces and nephews – I love you all.

To my dearest and closest friends, you have cheered me on in public and private.

To Pastor and Sister Bowen, you prayed for us and were physically at our sides often during this journey. To my church family, you prayed us through some of the darkest days and celebrated with us the sweetest victories.

To Pastor Bryan and Rhonda Matthews and Pastor Phillip and Amy Maxwell, thank you for your constant encouragement and the love you have shown to me and my family. I am thankful for the way God has grown our knowledge of the body of Christ in the last couple of years. We have added many new friends to our lives, and we are so appreciative of you all.

To Paula, Tanya, and Krista - As iron sharpens iron.

Endorsements

"All we can say is Wow! We are so excited to have been given the honor of reading this book by Holly Murray. Her book invites you into their journey of Caleb's story. You will feel up close and personal with her as she is candid about their highs and lows, mountains and valleys. You will find yourself caught up in their story as they are so transparent. I love how the entire family was included in this book and you hear from each family member what they were experiencing through Caleb's journey. Holly is one that writes out of a pure heart desiring no glory for herself. She reminds us of Nathan in the Bible - when Jesus saw him under the tree, He said that he is a man with no guile. This author is that caliber of a person! We love the fact that she has incorporated so much of the Word of God in this book, which has the power to change anyone's circumstances. We know you will be encouraged and transformed as you read this book."

-Bryan and Rhonda Matthews

Lead Pastors, New Life Church

Augusta Ga

"Victory is defined as a success or triumph over an enemy in battle or war, and was declared when Jesus rose from the grave. Jesus gave us the keys to the kingdom and each of us use the keys in different ways. The Murrays used the keys of faith, unity, and love to conquer life's greatest enemies - not cancer, but fear, doubt, and hopelessness.

Revelation 12:11 says, 'We overcome by the blood of the Lamb and the word of our testimony.' Let this story inspire you as God's Word empowers you to victory over life's ups and downs. We have the victory thru our Lord Jesus Christ!"

"Get ready for your miracle, it's your turn now! This book is full of a *true* life's story, packed with *true* Scriptures from a *true* Heavenly Father who loves *you*.

We are believing that as your fingers touch these pages and as your faith is built up by reading the Scriptures and Caleb's testimony, that healing is taking place right now in you. Psalm 107:20 says, 'He sent out His Word and healed them; He rescued them from the grave.' These pages are packed full of faith and truth from the Word of God that is ready to bring a swift shift and a miracle to your life now. Miracle after miracle, it's already yours!"

-Phillip and Amy Maxwell

Executive Pastors, New Life Church

Augusta Ga

“The wise man said, ‘There is no end to the writing of books, . . .’ (Ecclesiastes 12:12, GNT). It is therefore imperative that one pick and choose what to read. I often pick up a book and read a little here and there, after which I put it down and look for something else. Not so with this book! I was captured by the story and excited as I traveled through the pages. It was as though I was living with the Murray family. Read this book and pass it on to others, especially those dealing with the difficult challenges of life. This book is both informational and inspirational. Both thumbs up for the author and the story!”

-Rich Bowen

Senior Pastor, New Hope Worship Center

Augusta GA

“I am so glad that Jesus Christ still does miracles today. Caleb’s life and so many others stand as a witness that Jesus is who He says He is, and that He does what He says He can do. Let Him change your life today!”

-Lydia Marrow

Worship Leader,

Speaker and Writer/Editor

Shake the Nations Ministries,

Apopka, Florida and Rotherham, UK

Therefore, we never stop thanking God
that when you received His message from us,
you didn't think of our words as mere human
ideas. You accepted what we said as the very
Word of God – which, of course, it is.
And this Word continues to work
in you who believe.

1 Thessalonians 2:13 (NLT)

Contents

Introduction

I feel like I need to write a disclaimer. Like it needs to be in really big, super-large font. Maybe even stretched from corner to corner on this page. I HAVE NOT ARRIVED! I am so far from perfect that it isn't even mildly funny. Okay, maybe that's kinda funny. I do not have everything in my life all together. I have laundry waiting to be folded in the dryer, I see two leaves on the living room floor that need to be swept up, and I have dust on my piano and ceiling fan blades. My dogs are sleeping soundly on my sofa, and my children are off-task instead of cleaning their rooms. I have unanswered emails and other projects yet undone. Please tell me that this is what your life is sometimes like. This is my life, too. I sometimes lose my cool and (gasp) raise my voice in frustration to my children or make that chalkboard-scraping sigh that my husband just ADORES. Yes, that was sarcasm.

Despite all my imperfections, however, God delights in using me when I will say yes to His commands. Don't let me fool you. I don't always say yes when I hear His voice. Three summers ago, He "suggested" to me that I lead a ladies' connect group at church, and I very quickly shot that down with a resounding "no." I rationalized to God that I was very content helping the amazing leader of the group I attended every Thursday night. I loved the women in that group. I was connected there. They were my people. And it isn't that I didn't want more people, I just wanted them to be in the group of which I was already a part.

So, when God told me one Sunday morning to write a book, I really wanted to look around the empty room to see if there was someone else to whom He could possibly be speaking. He certainly couldn't mean me, could He? And yet, I was the only one there. And because He is not surprised by my hard-headedness, He confirmed it in multiple big and small ways over and over until I caught on that He was serious. So here I am. An author.

1

The Creativity of Grace

For the grace of God that brings salvation has appeared to all men, teaching us that, denying ungodliness and worldly desires, we should live soberly, righteously, and in godliness in this present world, as we await the blessed hope and the appearing of the glory of our great God and Savior Jesus Christ, who gave Himself for us, that He might redeem us from all lawlessness and purify for Himself a special people, zealous of good works. Teach these things, exhort, and rebuke with all authority. Let no one despise you.
Titus 2:11-15 (MEV)

God is so ultimately creative. He can choose to resolve a problem in a way that you would never have believed possible - in a way that you have never even heard of before. Whether your life seems relatively simple and everything is progressing as smoothly as a boat glides across a serene and peaceful lake, or things couldn't be more tumultuous; God's beautiful, creative gift of grace is available for you to receive.

My life was running fairly smoothly. Any problems I faced were so miniscule in comparison to what I heard others discussing as commonplace. In fact, I'd always believed I didn't have much of a testimony at all. Nothing very dramatic had ever happened in my life. I didn't have the depth of understanding when I was younger to realize that it was the very grace of God that was at work in my life that empowered me to make Godly choices that kept me from teetering on the edge of a rocky cliff.

For the Lord God is a sun and shield;
the Lord bestows grace and favor and honor; no good thing will He withhold from those who walk uprightly.
Psalm 84:11 (AMP)

My Life

My husband Keith and I had been happily married 15 years. We had two beautiful sons, Caleb and Joshua, who were three years apart in age. Caleb is the eldest. He tends to be my quiet child until he wants to really tell you about something. At that point, you might as well kick back because it's going to be a while before you get a word in edgewise. Joshua has the personality of his dad. Like Keith, he is the life of the party – friendly, chatty, and full of life.

I was in my eighth year of teaching in an elementary school classroom. I had been teacher of the year at my school the previous year. This year, I was grade chair for all of the first-grade teachers. I considered this both an honor and a privilege. I enjoyed the time we spent together planning and discussing ways we could better serve the students in our care in the meetings held in my classroom after school.

Keith and I had prayed about and decided to pull our two sons out of public school that year and to enroll them in an online public school. Doing so would enable Keith to oversee their work at home since most of his insurance business he could operate from behind his desk in the office located beside our house. I had homeschooled them myself for three years, including the time during which I was working on my Master's degree, so that wouldn't be too difficult for my husband to do, right?

Everything seemed to be going as planned. I was a highly successful educator who absolutely loved being in the classroom. I had conquered my fear of having adults in my classroom by inviting adults in my classroom - I had parent volunteers scheduled in my room every week and we were all enjoying the benefits of their involvement. My students were thriving, scores were incredible, my evaluations were outstanding, and I was making a difference doing what I loved.

Sure, I worked crazy-long hours. The custodial staff ran me out of my classroom nearly every evening so they could lock up the building, and my car was often the last one in the parking lot. I'd come home, throw something together for dinner (if my husband didn't already have it waiting for me - which he often did), and then go hole up in the bedroom with stacks of papers to grade, lesson plans to write, or items to create that would keep my classroom running beautifully and my students engaged the following day.

My weekends were spent cleaning house, catching up on laundry, and working on stuff for school. It had been this way every year I taught, except now I had two children of my own at home. I hated the feeling that I was neglecting my family. Surely I was fulfilling my calling, however, loving on all of these precious first graders every day and encouraging and laughing with those whom I had the privilege to call my colleagues. Keith was the role-model father, helping teach our boys, training them, encouraging them, loving on them. This was my life.

We were working together toward everything we felt was important. We were involved at church serving in the music ministry every Sunday. The children were involved in the youth group, and I attended a weekly ladies' group. We were living a very fulfilling, albeit busy life. Often, however, our perspective of the ideal life may look like a pretty picture but be far from the masterpiece God wants to create for us.

God, the creator of all wonderful things, has a plan that far exceeds the limitations of our best imaginings. He alone knows how to mold each experience of our life into something beautiful, even if the experience is less than pleasant. My favorite Scripture reads, "'For I know the plans I have for you,' declares the Lord, 'plans to prosper you and not to harm you, plans to give you hope and a future.'" (Jeremiah 29:11, NIV)

This verse had become life to me earlier in my journey to parenthood and would be one that would become life to me once again.

Our perspective of the ideal life may look like a pretty picture, but be far from the masterpiece God wants to create for us.

Our Beach Trip

A few days before the 2011 school year began, Keith surprised the boys and me with an impromptu beach trip. I love the beach. It's my favorite place in the entire world. I love the sound of the waves crashing on the shore and the salt-scented wind blowing my hair in wisps around my face. I love the sun beating down - warming every inch of me, and the seagulls flying around looking for anyone who might want to give them a piece of their bread crust. I love the feel of scrubbing my toes along the ocean floor looking for sand dollars, finding the perfect shells, and watching toddlers knock down castles their fathers have patiently and time-consumingly built. I like to feel the watery sand drizzle down my fingers as I watch a tower of sand build beneath my fingers while I sit just beyond the reach of the surf – knowing in a matter of a few minutes, the tide will come in and wash away what I have built. It becomes a joyful race to see how tall I can make the tower before the waves cause it to melt back into the shore again.

These reasons and so many more make the beach my favorite travel destination. My husband knows this. He loves the crisp air of the mountains in the fall, but he takes me to the beach because he loves me and wants to do whatever he can to keep me his happy, bubbly wife. How sweet is that kind of love?

Our beach trip was lovely in every way. We had friends who had been on vacation in Jacksonville and ended up in a hospital room there hours away from home, family, and friends. Their precious brown-haired daughter had just received an unexpected diagnosis of diabetes while they were on their trip. We chose Jacksonville as our beach destination so that we could visit them in the hospital.

Keith thinks of things like that, and I love that about him. Me, I know when something is the right thing for us to do because when he mentions it, I get this overwhelming sense of peace that makes me want to cry for joy. My pastor has at times referred to this "sixth sense" as one of God's gifts to women to which their husbands would be wise to be attentive. Keith is quite respectful of my sensitivities, so we were both feeling sure that Jacksonville was the destination that God had in mind for our trip.

Bear one another's burdens,
and so fulfill the law of Christ.
Galatians 6:2 (ESV)

We spent some time with our friends in that hospital room, encouraging them. I remember being so proud of my own two patient children, giving up a portion of a family trip without argument or complaint to love on dear friends from church. We spent time in that room entertaining and being entertained by hearty conversation about how God was moving even in a difficult situation and how He had come through with provision. We even shared some laughter together over old times we'd had as we watched the children play around us. The comradery we felt made the tiny room seem so much larger than the reality.

It feels good to encourage the people we love, to know that we leave them in better condition than we found them. We left the hospital, feeling at peace with the prayers we prayed and consolation we'd given, and enjoyed a remarkably fun couple of days at the beach before heading home in time for the new school year to begin.

It feels good to encourage the people we love, to know that we leave them in better condition than we found them.

It was in the car on that long drive home from the beach that our eleven-year-old son, Caleb, pointed out a rather pink-looking bumpy rash that had developed in a line on his left leg. It began from a spot just above his ankle and circled up behind his knee. After a few days, we noticed that the rash had not gone away, and we made an appointment with his doctor, who also happened to be a dear friend to our family. Caleb's doctor looked at it, and prescribed a cream to treat the rash. It didn't take long for his skin to clear up, but Caleb began to have a lot of pain in his left calf. It seemed to come and go - sometimes we would watch him limp down the stairs or pause and grab his leg when he was running through the grass in the field in front of our house.

We thought the pain might be related to the rash, and one afternoon the pain was so severe that Keith took Caleb to the ER while I stayed home with his younger brother. After an examination, the doctor felt that the pain Caleb was experiencing was not related to the rash, but likely growing pains based on his age and a recent growth spurt. Our family physician and good friend had recommended that an x-ray be performed, but the emergency room doctor believed that measure to be unnecessary, so Keith and Caleb returned home.

An Unexpected Trip

Two weeks later, on October 2, 2011, we were on our way to church. A typical Sunday morning for us has me waking to the most annoying sounds my phone can possibly offer at 5:30, with the goal set to be on the road by 6:30. This is no small feat, and much to my husband's chagrin, I often fall a bit short of the mark. It takes a bit of preparation the night before going anywhere for those of us who struggle in the art of decision making. I have developed that struggle to a fine art and will go to great lengths to avoid making decisions that affect others! It also takes a great deal of preparation to prevent the last-minute frantically asked questions like, "Where's my right shoe?" "Has anyone seen my belt?" "Do you have the deodorant?" so typical for my boys. But with a bit of hustling we manage to make it to church in time for vocal warm-up each week.

This particular Sunday morning was a little different, however. It began with a relatively quiet 45-minute drive to church. Each of my two young boys was undoubtedly occupied with his thoughts or buried in an electronic device of his choosing, while Keith and I listened to the inspiring music that would be played that morning in service. We had no idea that this quiet trip to church would be the start of the most difficult journey we have faced together.

Shortly before we arrived at church, we noticed Caleb crying in the backseat. He had been in a good bit of pain over the last few days, and nothing we had tried had proven to alleviate the pain as we helplessly watched him limp from place to place. His silent tears this Sunday morning, however, as he tried his best to endure the pain he was in, spurred us to action. Like his mom, he is one who hates to cry and prefers the "suffer in silence" train of thought. Knowing this made the fall of tears more alarming to us both.

Keith decided that we would go straight to the hospital ER in the hope of finding a solution to our son's pain. As my mind tried to wrap itself around all that I was seeing and hearing that morning, I told Keith that I felt it would be best if I dropped Joshua and him off at church and then take Caleb to the emergency room myself. I was fairly certain that there would be a long, miserable wait followed by a simple prescription that would solve the problem, and none of that would be improved by having all three of us waiting with Caleb. Besides, Keith was the band director at church, and his responsibilities and role were important. Keith agreed and we put the hastily laid plan to action.

The Plan

Have you ever had a moment when you thought you were strong enough to do something by yourself, or at least that you should be strong enough to do it? This was one of those moments for me. It seemed like it would be a series of fairly simple tasks. Drop Keith and Joshua off, enter the address of the hospital into my favorite GPS map, follow the step-by-step directions, and tell the doctors my son has been dealing with leg pain. Simple. I had no idea about the extent of grace that God was about to place in my possession. But God knew. He knew exactly how much grace I was going to require before I was aware that it would be needed.

Grace - that unearned gift of unmerited favor that empowers us to do and be all God has called us to be. That Sunday morning, God would gift me with the grace to keep my emotions in check as I received life-changing news while I sat stoically in the presence of my eleven-year-old in that tiny yellow confining room in the middle section of the ER.

God knows how much grace will be required of you before you are even aware that you will need any grace at all.

All during the sermon of the first service at church, Keith repeatedly checked his phone for a message on Caleb's progress. Undoubtedly, he wondered when he would hear from me. Many questions ran through his mind. When would I be back at church? Would I make it in time to sit beside him after the music at 11:00, as was our tradition? Did the doctors find the problem and have a solution in mind? Was Caleb okay? But these unasked questions were all left unanswered and he left his phone on the church seat to head to the platform and play during the altar time at the close of the first service.

After the first service, he headed with some of our friends to get the usual cup of steaming black coffee between services in the church gym. I always cherished that hour long break after the first service and before the second. It was a special time in which I was able to share my favorite drink with some of my nearest and dearest friends and discuss the interesting tidbits that were going on in our lives. There is really something special about Godly alliances. God creates people uniquely, and the resulting friendship becomes the beautiful golden thread that binds two completely different cuts of cloth in such a resplendent and remarkable way. Only such a loving Creator would design friendships this way, and we were blessed with some very special friends.

Friendship is the golden thread
that binds two completely different cuts of cloth
in such a remarkably beautiful fashion.

Settled in a chair surrounded by some of the people we love most in the world, Keith looked down at his phone to check for messages. The first one he saw was from me. It read, "Get down here now." Five remaining, closely-sent messages gave him the horrifying news that the doctors had found a growth on our son's leg. One of our best friends was sitting beside him as he read the messages, one after another, and she watched his expressions change. She was well aware that Keith was awaiting an update from me. I have no idea what she was thinking as she was looking at him, or if she has any idea how much her quick response to what she saw has meant to our family. She reached in her purse, grabbed her keys, handed them to Keith, and told him to take her car. Keith quickly located Joshua and drove faster than he probably should have to be by our side at the hospital as our life completely changed course.

I waited for my hero to come rescue me.

But He said to me, "My grace is sufficient for you,
for My strength is made perfect in weakness."
Therefore, most gladly I will boast in my weaknesses,
that the power of Christ may rest upon me.
2 Corinthians 12:9 (MEV)

2

The Storm Blows In

There will be a covering over every person.
This covering will be a place of safety.
It will protect the people from the heat of the sun.
It will be a safe place to hide from the storm and rain.
Isaiah 4:5b-6 (ICB)

Have you ever watched a dust devil blowing across a field on a hot summer day? I have, and I find them fascinating to watch. Andrea Thompson (2014) has written that these curiosities form when a portion of the ground heats faster than the surrounding area. This warmer air rises and pushes the surrounding cooler air aside. If the wind blows, it can shift this circulating air to its side and a dust devil is formed. If my boys and I spot a dust devil churning up a field when driving through our small town, we always make an effort to pull over to watch it wind over the furrowed hills and dance across the mounds of dirt until it dissipates.

Whirlwinds created by instabilities in our personal atmosphere can displace what is normal leaving our emotions swirling in their wake. Fear is a palpable emotion that the enemy of our soul delights in stirring within our minds. Many times, just when you feel that you have beaten back the cyclonic emotions, Satan sends a puff in your general direction that can stir up a storm again. He delights in keeping our minds captive to his assaults, and if we don't recognize what he is doing, we may succumb to the attack.

Whirlwinds created by instabilities in our personal atmosphere displace what is normal leaving our emotions swirling in their wake.

There was no question for my family. We had entered a war zone and the only thing I felt at that moment was shock and disbelief at the words I was hearing being thrown like bombs around me. As suppositions and conjectures from white-coated, stethoscope-wearing professionals were recklessly churning in the air, I gaped horrified at my young son who was lying on a slender bed robed in a thin light-blue cotton gown tied behind his neck with a worn, white cord. I could feel my husband at my side though I don't remember seeing him. My eyes saw nothing but my child and then he became blurry within my field of vision.

Jesus and the Storm

There's a story in Scripture that begins in Luke chapter eight. It speaks of a time when the disciples were heading across the Sea of Galilee. Scripture says that a "fierce storm came down on the lake" (Luke 8:22 NLT). Because of the geography of the area around the Sea of Galilee, storms can arise violently and with no warning. Though this particular storm caught the disciples by surprise, Jesus was not alarmed at the suddenness and violence of the storm. Nor was He worried about the outcome. He knew there would be a storm. He knows everything, and getting into the boat to head across the lake had been His plan from the beginning! Verse 22 reads, "One day Jesus said to His disciples, 'Let's cross to the other side of the lake.' So they got into a boat and started out" (Luke 8:22 NLT). I'm confident that Jesus knew an important lesson would result from this storm blowing in.

Make no mistake; the storm they were facing was a serious situation. The Bible says, "The boat was filling with water, and they were in real danger" (Luke 8:23 NLT). But going to the other side of the lake had been Jesus's idea. He knew that He would be in the boat when the storm came and that His presence would be all that the disciples would need to face the raging tempest.

The disciples were, in essence, freaking out. They immediately verbalized the worst conclusion as their impending reality. Their cry when waking Jesus from sleep (yes, He was at complete peace even in the storm) was, "Master, Master, we're going to drown!" (Luke 8:24 NLT). They saw no other conclusion. The storm was that bad. But Jesus woke, rebuked the storm, and the storm obeyed His voice. I can imagine that His next words fell upon their ears louder than any thunder they had ever heard, "Where is your faith?" (Luke 8:25, NLT).

Peace in the Storm

The presence of God calms such turbulent atmospheric conditions, and God was certainly with me in the ER that morning. I did not break down into sobs or collapse into a chair. I stood. It was as though Jesus was holding my body up and keeping the violence of the storm raging around me from impacting my body in a way that would be completely natural. He was controlling the inside of me - bringing peace to the turmoil and keeping the effects of the storm at bay.

Like the storm the disciples faced, we were facing an incredibly serious situation. It was every inch a whirlwind. Within minutes of hearing that there was a growth, doctors ordered x-rays, an MRI, CT scan, and a bone scan - all to take place that same day. They scheduled a surgery for the following day - a biopsy, so that they would know exactly what they were dealing with. They were fairly certain the growth was a tumor, most likely cancer. Cancer. I wanted to scream, "But he is only eleven-years old!!!!" It didn't feel like anyone was asking my permission to complete all of these tests on my son, though we did have to sign consent forms for every procedure. Bundling him up and driving the hour-trip home from the hospital was not really an option I was given. It definitely was not the recommendation. Instead, I walked with my husband and youngest son at my sides behind the wheelchair that was carrying my eldest - from one area of the hospital to another - clueless about what direction we were headed. Yet somehow God gave me the strength to keep walking.

His strength is perfect when our strength is gone.
He'll carry us when we can't carry on.
Raised in His power the weak become strong.
His strength is perfect.
His strength is perfect.
(Steven Curtis Chapman, 1988)

Pressure

When measuring atmospheric pressure, the higher up you go, the less pressure there is. The pressure mounted as we waited at the hospital. We were bombarded by fears that attacked our peace. Scripture instructs us in James 4:8 that if we will draw close to God, He will draw close to us. This verse immediately follows "Resist the devil and he will flee from you" (James 4:7, NKJV). We relied on God's Word to lower our personal pressure. Scripture, coupled with the prayers, presence, and encouragement of our family and friends, is how we survived those first few days, weeks, and months to follow.

As Caleb recovered in the hospital from the biopsy of the mass in his left leg, a surgeon called Keith and me into a room filled with a long, dark, wooden conference table surrounded with chairs. Keith and I sat side by side, each clinging to the hand of the other. The sunshine beaming through the windows lining the far wall called to me to go outside, but I shifted my focus to the serious-looking surgeon and a petite, white-coated lady standing with him. She looked so kind. Her voice was so gentle that it was nearly inaudible. As she spoke words that I strained to hear, the news exploded in my ears - it was cancer.

There were many words that day. Most of them I did not understand. Nothing in my years of previous study or time spent caring for my young family prepared me for hearing the earth-shattering terminology. The oncologist began to tell about some of the procedures that lay ahead of us. Everything in me screamed to tell them all to stop talking! This could not be happening. This could not be real. When they finally fell silent, I could feel the pressure of my husband's hand on mine. I locked my large blue eyes on his indomitable face and serious brown eyes. Keith spoke.

"This is where the rubber meets the road. We have been learning about faith and talking about faith for years. Now is when we put our faith to work. We don't have another choice," he said. I remember that I didn't particularly want to hear those words in that moment. I wanted to hear that there was nothing wrong, that there had been a crazy misunderstanding, and we could go home right away.

But those were words I would not hear that day. Instead, the words of truth penetrated my mind. I had to believe that everything I knew about the Lord was true – that He loved me and my family, that He would never leave me, and that He would provide for every need we would ever face.

This is where the rubber meets the road.
We have been learning about faith
and talking about faith.
Now is when we put our faith to work.
We don't have another choice.

Keith was right. We had both been reared in church and knew the Word. Our pastor had taught us for years about the importance of faith and using the Word of God as the invincible sword to pierce through personal attacks. I felt the influence of the armor of God on me instead of the weight of the diagnosis, and with resolve I squared my shoulders.

Grace

This kind of boldness is God-given. It's grace. In Romans, Paul speaks to his fellow believers, saying, "Nevertheless, brothers, I have written even more boldly to you on some points, to remind you, because of the grace that is given to me from God" (Romans 15:15, MEV). Grace is a gift freely given, but it gives a boldness to stand firmly, unwaveringly on the Truth of His Word. We had no other choice other than dog-headed, unfaltering, unshakable faith that God would do what His Word said He would do. We could not - would not - lose our son. That was not a possibility that we could even consider for a moment.

All of the tests the local doctors had run on the tumor that was biopsied were giving contradictory results. They were uncertain the type of cancer that we faced. We clung to this small glimmer of hope like a lifeline while the doctors shipped the lab work off to the Mayo Clinic. My mind awaited a phone call that would inform us that their original cancer diagnosis was incorrect, and that everything would be as it was before the pain began. We asked our family and friends to join us in praying for Caleb, and we began looking up and quoting Scriptures that promised healing.

Like a ship tossed up and down on the waves, our emotions fluctuated from fear to confidence and back again as we battled the relentless mental attacks from the enemy with the Word of God. But the Lord knew that we would all face storms of one kind or another in life. Even the disciples had to have known that there was a chance they could see a violent storm on the Sea of Galilee. It was not an uncommon occurrence because of the geography of the area and they were seasoned fishermen. Scripture says, "These things I have spoken to you, that in Me you may have peace. In the world you will have tribulation; but be of good cheer, I have overcome the world" (John 16:33, NKJV). Jesus didn't tell us that we would have trouble to make us afraid. He spoke this for quite different reasons. He delights in our having the confidence in His ability to take care of us when we face situations that we cannot deal with on our own. We just must have faith that His Word is true.

Faith

You might wonder, "What do you mean, 'have faith'?". Scripture defines faith for us in Hebrews 11:1, reading, "Faith is the confidence that what we hope for will actually happen; it gives us assurance about things we cannot see" (NLT). It is confidently knowing, trusting, that what His Word says is true is absolutely true and will come to pass exactly as He said it would. And everyone has faith. In Romans 12:3, the Apostle Paul states, "For I say, through the grace given to me, to every man that is among you, not to think of himself more highly than he ought to think, but to think soberly, according as God hath dealt to every man the measure of faith" (NKJV). You see God gave every single person the measure of faith.

So how much faith is "the measure?" It is the measure that you need at the time you need it. It takes faith to receive salvation. Ephesians 2:8-9 reads, "For by grace you have been saved through faith, and that not of yourselves, it is the gift of God, not of works, lest anyone should boast" (NKJV).

You don't have to work to achieve a tremendous measure of faith to receive salvation. Just as salvation is a gift, so are the faith and grace required to receive it. If we had to work to earn faith, then we would be able to brag in the amount of faith that we had or be able to brag that we had earned salvation itself, and that is contrary to the Word of God. Faith is confidence in God doing what He said He would do.

How much faith is "the measure" of faith
that you have been given?
It is the amount you need at the time you need it.

As you become more familiar with what He says He will do (by reading His Word) and as you gain more experience in His faithfulness by walking in relationship with Him, your confidence in Him grows. Pastor Bill Johnson (2017) spoke to this same faith in a message he gave on January 29, 2017, saying, "Faith is actually the most normal response to the discovery of who He is, because all it is is a confidence in His nature, in His Word." Later in this same message on the topic of faith, he also said, "Faith is being overwhelmingly confident that He is who He says He is" (Johnson, 2017).

As your confidence in Him grows, your faith grows. And it doesn't take a mountain of faith to see God work in amazing ways. In Matthew 17:20, Jesus says, "'I tell you the truth. If your faith is as big as a mustard seed, you can say to this mountain, 'Move from here to there.' And the mountain will move. All things will be possible for you'" (ICB).

I once bought a small container of mustard seed from my local grocery store. When I got home, I took one of the seeds out and held it in my hand. You should try this. It is a very real thing that you can touch – something specific that Jesus talked about. And it is tiny. That is how much faith I needed to move my mountain.

The longer you walk with God, looking for the ways He is moving in your life and the lives around you, the more your confidence and faith in God will grow. I am glad that God knew we would need faith and that He gave it to us all, because Hebrews 11:6 states, "Now without faith it is impossible to please God, for the one who draws near to Him must believe that He exists and rewards those who seek Him" (HCSB).

Where is Your Faith?

After stilling the stormy waters for the disciples, Jesus responded, "Where is your faith?" (Luke 8:25, MEV). He asks the same thing of us when the storms of life threaten to capsize our own vessels. "Where is your faith, My child?" He asks.

Sometimes I think it is easier to have faith when you don't know anything - when nothing directly contradicts that for which you are hoping and praying. Ten days after the biopsy, we were still waiting on the results to come back from the Mayo Clinic. Caleb was recovering nicely from surgery. We were praying and quoting Scripture constantly. I was back at work teaching first graders, and the boys were back in the books at home.

Keith and I were delighted that Caleb was no longer experiencing leg pain, other than the pain from the stitches pulling occasionally. In a meeting with the orthopedic surgeon who had removed the bone sample for testing, Keith shared this news. The orthopedic surgeon seemed surprised by this detail. He said that sometimes opening an area would relieve pressure and ease pain, but not usually in the case of tumors. He could not tell us that we were not dealing with a tumor, but that it would be unusual for the pain to ease if it was a tumor. He refused to speculate further until the pathology reports came back. Another message of hope buoyed us and Keith shared the news with those who were praying with us. He began a blog as an easy way to communicate updates to all of our family and friends and as a way to keep record of the miracles for which we believed.

We knew miracles were possible, and it wasn't just because we had read about them in the Bible. Our pastor's wife told us a story years ago about how she prayed over her children when she was expecting them. That was a piece of information at the time that I tucked back in my mind to use when Keith and I decided to begin a family of our own. So when the day came that I discovered I was expecting Caleb (before I knew this baby would be a Caleb) I began to pray. I prayed some of the things my pastor's wife had prayed over her unborn children - I prayed for my child's salvation, for their future spouse, but I added something different. For this child, I prayed that God would bless them with an amazing musical gift that they could use for the Lord.

The Gift

When Caleb was born, he didn't come with an instruction manual or a saxophone like his dad played. He was 8 pounds, 6.8 ounces of pure preciousness, but as I looked adoringly at this baby in my arms, I saw nothing at all that indicated that those things for which I had prayed would come to pass. Some miracles are like that - they are there; you just don't know it yet. We can't always see God's hand at work in our life. That doesn't mean He isn't working. As Caleb got older, we began to notice some things about him that made it clear that God had heard and answered my months of praying.

Some miracles are like that –
they are there; you just don't know it yet.

Let's back up more than 30 years. I took piano lessons for seven years. I hated it - really hated it. But as a result of much training, I can play - very little. I do, however, have some basic theory understanding and am fairly adept at reading the treble clef. That was very fortunate for me, because when I started dating Keith (who is a master musician) he agreed to teach me how to play the flute. Hurray! Private lessons on how to pucker my lips! That is just what I wanted to learn! Even as I write this, I am laughing quite loudly and blushing profusely! I mean my parents and best friends are going to read this! Sorry Keith, but it is true!

I was a mediocre flautist. I enjoyed it, but I really had to work hard and get extra lessons from my instructor to be skilled enough to play in my church orchestra. After a couple of years of private instruction, I was okay enough to be asked to play in special programs at other churches. I thought I had arrived.

Fast-forward to Caleb, who on the other hand walked up to our piano at around three or four years of age and began to pick out songs rather proficiently. I don't just mean *Mary had a Little Lamb*, either. He was picking out songs that he had heard his dad and me rehearse for church choir. Caleb did not get his musical skills from his mom. To help him understand more about music, Keith ordered a piano book and began to work with him on basic notes and teaching him to play the piano.

It was around this time that we noticed another strong and unusual gifting in Caleb as well. I like to sing. Since my flute-playing days were long since over, I sang in the choir and on the praise team at church. Keith and I often spend a lot of time listening to and singing along with music in the car, especially since we live such a long way from town.

One particular day we were coming home from church and listening to "Hear Our Praises" by Hillsong. This song is in the key of C, which means that there are no sharps or flats. Basically, you play all the white keys on the piano. While this song was playing through the cd player in the car, Caleb asked his dad if he remembered that song that he taught him on the piano. He began singing two notes back and forth to us. The notes he was singing clashed badly with the music to which we were listening, but Keith recognized that the notes Caleb was singing out sounded exactly like the notes in the song he'd been working with him on in the piano book he'd bought for Caleb.

We were almost home, so we quickly turned off the music that was playing and repeatedly sang the two notes Caleb had sung to us. Keith pulled down the driveway, threw the car in park, hastily unlocked the front door, and we ran to the piano to finger the keys and locate the notes Caleb had sung. We were absolutely amazed - he was correct. The exact two notes he had sung were the two in the book – at the exact pitch.

While this may not sound particularly phenomenal to some people, let me explain which two notes he sang. We were listening to the key of C. The two notes he sang (back and forth) were B flat, A flat, B flat. These notes are not normally played in a simple worship tune written in the key of C, which is why they clashed so badly with what we were singing. But even though a different key was being played, he could still identify with his perfect ears the two correct notes in the correct pitch at the same time.

Keith was shocked at this skill and began to test him on other songs, asking him to sing this song or that song.

Each time Caleb sang the notes he remembered hearing in the songs, Keith would check it on the piano and Caleb was singing the correct notes at the correct pitch every time. Keith is a brilliant musician, but he cannot do this. It cannot be taught. It is truly a gift from God.

When Caleb turned eight-years old, Keith and I purchased a beautiful, white Ibanez electric guitar complete with amp and headphones. The headphones were for my benefit. Gathered under the lighted carport at my parent's house, we watched him tear the brightly colored paper to reveal the gift we had chosen for him. His eyes were nearly as large as his excited grin. Within three years, he was easily playing along with many of the songs that we used at church and he loved picking the lead line on *Sweet Home Alabama* by Lynyrd Skynyrd.

It wasn't long before Caleb was mesmerizing everyone with his skills. Absolute pitch is the technical name for what he could do. It basically means that without a reference point, a person can sing or name a note or key that is heard. Caleb can even do this if a different song is being played - he is not confused in the slightest by the difference in sounds. This is not the same skill as simply matching a tone heard. Keith is a brilliant musician – I have already stated this. He has composed and transposed music, written parts for numerous instruments, and written his own songs. He has traveled the world playing a variety of instruments. In fact, he can play every instrument he has ever tried to play. But even he cannot do what Caleb can do. It's a very rare gift. Caleb did not get his mad musical skills entirely from his daddy. They came from his Heavenly Father. It was the gifting for which I had prayed.

The Results

Isn't it funny that just when you begin to realize an amazing gift from the Father, the enemy comes to disrupt your life and steal your joy? John 10:10 reads, "The thief comes only to steal and kill and destroy; I came that they may have life, and have it abundantly" (NASB). We knew that God would not and did not cause Caleb to have a growth on his leg. Tumors, cancer, any kind of sickness - those are not things that God does. It is the thief, the enemy, Satan who seeks to steal and destroy the good things with which God blesses us. When the enemy stirs a storm in your life, God's grace will allow you to speak peace to calm it. Use His Word to calm those storms.

When the enemy stirs a storm in your life, God's grace will allow you to speak peace to calm it.

October 19, 2011. In scrolling through Wikipedia, there is nothing especially significant that occurred on this day. For us, however, it was a pretty important day. We had been waiting for 16 days for the biopsy results. The days had felt like a lifetime to me while we waited, and the results had been due four days prior. I went to school. Keith had the boys situated with their school day. The day progressed as it usually did, and after school I began tidying my classroom, rearranging desks exited quickly by excited seven-year-olds ready to get their daily out-the-door hug from their teacher and be on their way home. I had completed these tasks with a smile. I then sat down at my desk to filter through the stacks of papers to be checked over when my classroom intercom buzzed, and the secretary alerted me to a phone call awaiting me in the office. I smiled and looked around my room to see which lunchbox or jacket may have been left hanging on the back of a desk that would prompt a phone call from a parent. Seeing nothing out of the ordinary, I told the secretary that I was on my way. I grabbed my grade book and a pencil, and walked down the brightly lit hallway with gleaming floors toward the office.

Upon entering the school office, lined with cheerful windows on two sides, I headed toward the secretary's desk to pick up the line. Placing a smile on my face that I hoped would reach the other side, I spoke, "Hello, this is Mrs. Murray." The voice that greeted me was one I recognized immediately, but the tone of voice frightened me. My mind was reeling. I know my cell phone had not rung. I had not missed a call. Why was Keith calling me at school? He NEVER called me at work. Then it occurred to me. This was an emergency.

3

Be Careful Little Mouth What You Say

Now may the God of hope fill you with all joy and peace in believing, so that you may abound in hope, through the power of the Holy Spirit.
Romans 15:13 (MEV)

The news was not that for which we had prayed. I knew that now. I didn't know every intricate detail; I only knew that Keith was coming for me. My car was parked in the space reserved for me close to the double-door entrance to the elementary school where I taught, but there it would stay.

The secretary had left her desk to give me a modicum of privacy while I received the phone call from Keith. She had recognized his voice, too. I returned the phone to the cradle and turned to head back to my classroom. I had to leave. I had to grade papers. I had work to do. I couldn't stay here. My classroom. I had to make it to my classroom. Hold it together. Hold it together.

I made it down the main hallway and halfway down my classroom's hallway before anyone noticed me. It was one of my closest friends. She saw my face. It must have read like a horror film. She grabbed me. She was talking but I couldn't understand what she was speaking. Within moments I felt another body beside me. It was my principal. The secretary had told her of Keith's call.

Tears were falling. I stuttered and stumbled over my explanations of what I needed to do in my classroom. The papers. I had papers to check. I needed to make lesson plans for the substitute - I would be out tomorrow. We have a meeting - the oncologist had finally called.

I could feel my colleagues embrace me as my body shook. Then my principal turned my body toward my classroom and helped me gather my things. My desk - everything was left right there. No papers left its surface. All I had in my hands was my purse and the beautiful blue and brown book bag containing my grade book. Years of training not failing me - always take your grade book and whistle with you. I still carry that whistle.

I was in my room less than two minutes before my principal was walking back up the brightly lit hallway with me at her side. All of my friends standing in their classroom doorways watched mournfully as I walked by them toward the office with my principal's arm supporting me. There was no wait time. Keith's gray Suburban was at the school doors when I opened them. I opened the passenger door and slid into the seat beside Keith. My principal shut the door behind me and uttered words that I didn't hear. I looked behind me at my silent children who were both watching me, and the tears continued to fall.

The Long Ride

I don't remember if Keith told me where we were going. It was probably the longest period of time I'd ever been quiet while awake and in a place where talking is usually not a problem. I was no longer shaking, but the tears were falling one after another. I did not speak one word. My teeth clamped my tongue firmly, and remained that way for the duration of the drive. Keith held my left hand. I could feel him rubbing circles with his thumb on the top of my hand and the pressure from an occasional squeeze. That was how I marked that time passed. I saw nothing. My right hand gripped the door's armrest. The atmosphere in the truck was tense and silent. I knew that if I loosened the grip my teeth had on my tongue, I would scream. I could feel it. So I just held on.

Forty-five minutes later, we pulled into the rear parking lot of our church. Our pastor was at the back door waiting for us. My two boys sat in the reception area quietly while our beloved pastor led us to his office.

I wish I could remember what he told us while I wept. I am certain that it was the most comforting words imaginable - full of hope and promise. I am sure he told us that God was not surprised by the news that had rocked us to the core. That He loved us and as Caleb's creator, He loved Caleb as well.

I'm certain that he told us he would be praying for us, and that if we needed anything to call him. I'm certain that he read Scripture and told us to hold tightly to the Lord and He would see us through. I remember that he prayed. I remember that was what I needed. I remember that the tears stopped flowing.

The words from the oncologist the following day were not as comforting. The official report was back from the Mayo Clinic. The diagnosis was Ewing's Sarcoma. It is a rare form of cancer that is mostly found in preteens, and mostly in boys, and according to Dr. David Derrer (2014), accounts for only about 1% of childhood cancers. Caleb's doctors wanted to do a PET scan within the week to make certain there were no other tumors they had missed in previous scans, and would follow that with an EKG so they would know the condition of his heart before chemotherapy began. They explained that some of the medicines he would be given could affect his heart's healthy condition and they would need to monitor it often. They planned to surgically install a port in his chest area so that an aggressive chemotherapy could begin immediately.

Another surgery. And this operation would be a delicate one. He hadn't completely healed from his last surgery. The doctors showed us what a port looked like, and pointed out the catheter that would run up into one of the larger veins in his neck that would support the chemotherapy drugs that would destroy lesser veins. They showed us the special needles that would be inserted into the port so that he could more easily receive the strong medicines that would hopefully kill the cancer cells and save his life.

Our Words

Keith again updated the blog. He loaded it down with Scripture after Scripture and implored our family and friends to join us in prayer for Caleb's healing. Scripture says, "Plans succeed through good counsel; don't go to war without wise advice" (Proverbs 20:18, NLT). We made plans for Caleb's care, but believed firmly that God would bring healing. We sought counsel from our family, our pastor, our closest friends, and the doctors. We went to war with a two-edged sword, the Word of God. It was during this time that we began to go beyond merely quoting healing Scripture aloud. We began to monitor very carefully the words that we spoke in regard to our situation.

Do you remember that childhood song, "O be Careful Little Eyes What You See?" I remember singing that in church when I was a child and singing it to my pupils as a Sunday school teacher when I was a little older. One of the stanzas in the song is "O be careful little mouth what you say. O be careful little mouth what you say. For the Father up above is looking down in love, so be careful little mouth what you say."

Psalm 141:3 reads, "Set a guard, O Lord, over my mouth; keep watch over the door of my lips!" (ESV). From the New Testament, "I tell you, on the day of judgment people will give account for every careless word they speak" (Matthew12:36, ESV). You see, the words we speak are powerful, and our Father is keenly aware of each one we utter. This song, instilled in our youngest children, is founded on the Word of God.

The words we speak are powerful,
and our Father is keenly aware of each one we utter.

Admonition to be careful with the words we speak is found throughout one of my favorite books of the Bible, Proverbs - the book of wisdom. Proverbs 12:18 reads, "There is one whose rash words are like sword thrusts, but the tongue of the wise brings healing" (ESV). Proverbs 18:7 reads, "A fool's mouth is his destruction, and his lips are the snare of his soul" (MEV). Verse twenty-one from that same book and chapter, "Death and life are in the power of the tongue, and those who love it will eat its fruit" (MEV).

These are not the only verses in Scripture that caution us to be careful with the words we choose to say. Scripture is full of reminders of the value of choosing our words wisely. Ephesians 4:29 reads, "Let no corrupting talk come out of your mouths, but only such as is good for building up, as fits the occasion, that it may give grace to those who hear" (ESV). So the words we speak - that build us up and encourage us - can give us grace? Grace - that gift from God, the power He bestows that provides both boldness and strength to do what

God calls you to do - and the words we speak will give grace to the listener? Yes! Yes, it does!

Dictionary.com defines *encourage* as “to inspire with courage, spirit, or confidence” (n.d.). Encouragement builds people up, inspires them to boldness, and gives them confidence. Godly encouragement reminds us of that God-given grace to confidently and courageously face life’s storms. So taking God at His Word, recognizing it as the Truth that it is, we paid attention to every possible detail of the words that we spoke over our son or about our son.

We were careful never to say it was “Caleb’s tumor,” for example. The illness that was attacking his body didn’t belong there and it didn’t belong to him. God didn’t create Caleb with it - it was nothing that was good. And it wasn’t anything that we wanted him to have. So it was “the tumor”, “the cancer”, and “the sickness” that we came against with our words. Keith wrote in his blog to those following to please keep bad news or bad reports of similar situations to themselves. He also requested that they only speak words of healing and life over our son, whether they were talking to us or not.

We even avoided the popular expression, “you’re killing me.” Does that sound like an extreme measure? Perhaps. But this was too serious a battle to consider not fighting with every weapon in our possession. We were constantly on the lookout for more weaponry to add to our arsenal to fight. 2 Corinthians 10:4 reads, “For the weapons of our warfare are not carnal, but mighty through God to the pulling down of strongholds" (MEV). This was not a time to hold back. When you are fighting for something important, you give it all you know to give, and you don't stop until the battle is over and victory is yours.

This was too serious a battle to consider not fighting with every weapon in our possession.

Praise

Along with praying Scripture that promised healing and brought encouragement and being careful with our word choices, we also came against the enemy with praise. Praise is a powerful weapon and sometimes it feels like the hardest weapon to use.

There is something about music that touches the very deepest parts of us and stirs our emotions. When we listen to fast, cheerful music, it makes us want to move and dance. Movies use music to help build suspense or even move us to tears of joy or sadness, depending on the mood of the sounds we hear. Teachers use music to help children learn and remember concepts. A study by John Hopkins University discusses that different types of music help us with recall, improve concentration, expand our thinking skills, help us improve creativity, increase productivity, make activities more fun, and relax us (Brewer, 1995).

I've often heard it said that it is easy to praise the Lord when you are on the mountaintop - when everything is going your way. I have found that to be true myself. When everyone is getting along, there's plenty in the bank, your refrigerator and cupboards are full, your family and friends are in good health and happy, your marriage is blissful, the house is clean - yes, when you're surrounded by amazing things for which to be thankful, it is easy to sing bright songs of praise to God, to speak of His goodness and worth.

But what about when times are hard? What about the times when there is no milk in the refrigerator or bread in the pantry? Or when the phone rings and there is a bill collector on the other end? What about times when your children aren't even speaking to you, you're distant to your own relatives or friends, or you and your spouse aren't communicating anymore? What if you are facing an illness, your child is sick, or there is some other storm in your life? Is praising God easy then? Is He still good? Is He still worthy of our praise?

Praising may not be easy when we are focused on difficult situations, but yes, He is still good and He is still worthy of praise. God never changes, nor does His love for us wane. Psalm 107:1 reads, "Give thanks to the Lord, for He is good; His faithful love endures forever" (MEV).

Sacrifice

Scripture speaks of a sacrifice of praise in Hebrews. "Through Him, therefore, let us at all times offer up to God a sacrifice of praise, which is the fruit of lips that thankfully acknowledge *and* confess *and* glorify His name" (Hebrews 13:15, AMP). The word sacrifice as used in this verse, according to the Blue Letter Bible (n.d.), comes from the Greek word "thysia" (pronounced thu-se-a), which is defined "to kill, sacrifice, or slay."

Sacrifice is defined at Dictionary.com as "the surrender or destruction of something prized or desirable for the sake of something considered as having a higher or more pressing claim" (n.d.). So what is the thing that we are surrendering to God or destroying, laying down in exchange for praising Him? Jack Hayford (2015a) puts it this way, "We 'kill' our pride, fear, or sloth - anything that threatens to diminish or interfere with our worship of the Lord." Because regardless of what we face, battle, or fear, or what makes us angry or brings pain, God is still worthy of our worship and adoration. He sacrificed His Son, Jesus, for us. Jesus gave his very life in exchange for ours so that we may, through that sacrifice, receive salvation and one day spend eternity with Him. All we have to do is ask Him to save us. Romans 10:9 (NKJV) reads, "If you confess with your mouth the Lord Jesus and believe in your heart that God has raised Him from the dead, you will be saved." It is really that simple. When you are in a battle, let your words of praise to your Savior demolish your fears. Our words have power, and that sacrifice of praise is a powerful exchange.

When you are in a battle,
let your words of praise to God demolish your fears.

War

Our war commenced. The day for the surgery came and the port was placed. Our family surrounded us during the surgery as we all prayed that the delicate surgery would be successful. There were prayers. There were tears. There was pressure. But there was God, and we felt the Holy Spirit's presence calm our nerves and bring peace. We weren't alone in any way.

Caleb's doctors told us they would begin chemotherapy after the surgery, and I presumed they meant after his incisions from surgery healed. I was under the wrong impression. The following evening was our first introduction to chemotherapy. Both Keith and I were fairly familiar with the doctors, nurses, and hospital layout, so when it began to get late I suggested Keith take Joshua and go to his parents' house in town so that he could get some rest.

There was a chair, a sofa bed, and a trundle that were in the room with Caleb, but it was very crowded and quite uncomfortable for all four of us to spend the night in the room. I couldn't bring myself to not be there for Caleb on his first chemotherapy procedure. If I had taken Joshua and gone to my in-laws' house for the night, my imagination would have been very hard to contain. I just had to be with my son. I was confident that I could manage his first night of chemotherapy on my own, but Keith made me promise to call him if I needed anything.

I remember when the nurse entered the room bearing the bags of chemo. She had several bags with her and a special gown that I had never seen the nurses wear before. She put on a pair of different colored gloves than the nurses had been using when they would examine Caleb. The painstaking way she was preparing everything made her look as though she was preparing for the most dangerous of tasks.

The atmosphere in the room was tense. I began to feel very fearful. She asked me if there was any possibility that I was expecting a child. I told her there was none. She began to explain that the medicine she was about to administer to my child was extremely potent and that I must not get any on my skin. She explained further that it would probably make him sick and that I must not get any emesis on my skin either. She showed me the gown and gloves that I would need to put on before assisting him if he became ill. I was beginning to feel a sense of panic descend.

She had a tall blue bucket that had a liner in it for Caleb to use in the event it was needed. It looked like it belonged on a beach and not in a hospital room, but we were a long way from such carefree days as that. She placed the bucket on the tall mobile tray beside his bed and laid a handful of liners beside it. This indicated to me that she anticipated Caleb would need more than one.

I watched the nurse lay out a series of sterile equipment on top of a small blue plastic sheet. She was being very careful in the way she opened each item and I watched her carefully and thoroughly scrub each connection with a fresh alcohol wipe before inserting the needles connected to the tubing that led to the bag of medicine hanging on the long metal IV stand. Everything looked and felt very different now than all of my hospital experiences to date. Fear and panic were definitely settling in my mind. As my heart raced and breathing became faster, I reached for my cell phone and dialed Keith's number.

He had not been gone from the hospital very long at all, but I could tell that I had woken him. He groggily but hurriedly asked me what was wrong. I told him the nurse had come in and hooked Caleb to his first round of chemo. He could hear the panic in my voice and told me he was on his way. I couldn't argue. I was terrified. The nurse had so heavily warned me of the dangers of touching my child that her voice drowned all my confidence in a sea of fear. One big puff from the enemy, and just like that the storm had swiftly and unexpectedly plummeted on my consciousness.

The First Night

We made it through that first of many sleepless chemotherapy nights. Keith was on the uncomfortable bed against the large windows and I was curled into the chair beside Caleb's bed. Nurses came often, and machines beeped steadily as medicine was pumped into the body of my eleven-year-old son.

Caleb became very sick, and used the bucket often. I became very fast at suiting up that first night, gown backwards covering my clothes, gloves, grab the rag, wash the rag, wipe sweet Caleb, rinse, never let any part the medicine-infused vomit touch any part of his skin or mine - careful, careful, careful. Discard rag, seal and discard lining of bucket in the proper receptacle, replace liner, get a fresh rag, discard gloves, rehang gown, check on Caleb, lay back down. This routine repeated itself often over the next few days.

I cannot tell you what a miracle my handling any of this was. I have never handled throwing up well. When I was pregnant with each of my boys I was terribly sick. It was an all-day-long, 9-months-long kind of sick. During the beginning of my pregnancy with Caleb, my obstetrician had tried many medicines and was preparing to use a pump to administer a consistent dose of nausea-prevention medicine until we found a medicine that helped me fight the strongest symptoms.

While I've heard most expectant moms gain weight with their babies, I lost weight when pregnant with mine. With Caleb, I lost twenty pounds, and he was more than eight pounds himself. I used to joke that if I could just stay pregnant all the time, I'd be as skinny as a rail! One of my first lucid thoughts after delivering Caleb as I laid in the hospital bed looking over at my son in the plastic nursery bassinet was, "I'm not sick!" I had been sick for so long, I guess I figured I would always feel sick.

I went through exactly the same things when I was pregnant with Joshua that I had been through when I was expecting Caleb, so my doctor hastily prescribed the medicine that had proven effective with my first pregnancy. I made it through the pregnancy and delivered a healthy, bouncing 10 pounds and 4-ounce baby boy. He was the talk of the hospital nursery.

Keith was the ideal husband through both pregnancies, taking excellent care of his very nauseated wife. It didn't matter where I was; he cleaned up behind me if I didn't make it to the bathroom in time. I just couldn't do it. The thought of having to clean that up - and I shudder at the memories - was unconscionable. But Keith was exactly the same way with our children. If dry heaving began, it was Keith to the rescue. Poopy diapers, and I was your girl. Throwing up, though - that was all Keith.

So now my son, weak with nausea and hooked to numerous tubes and bags, was not capable of making it to the bathroom himself. But God is so miraculous. He freely gives us the grace - the strength and power - to do what needs to be done, even in the most difficult of situations. He did not fail me here, and His strength was made perfect in my weakness.

Caleb was to endure 5 days of chemotherapy in the hospital and would follow that with 3-4 days of traveling to the oncology clinic for additional treatments. This would be the expected pattern, repeated for many months. He would be given a variety of medicines to attack the cancerous cells in his body, on a very intense schedule.

God was already proving Himself faithful in so many ways, just as He had been our whole life. We were weak at times, and He held us up. We cried, and His Spirit brought comfort. Our family was by our side often, and our friends rallied and prayed with us as well. We prayed, we sang, and we fought the battle every way that we knew how to fight.

4

God Moves in His Timing

But those who wait upon the Lord
shall renew their strength;
they shall mount up with wings as eagles,
they shall run and not be weary,
and they shall walk and not faint.
Isaiah 40:31 (MEV)

There are times in my life when I can be incredibly patient. I waited patiently to get married while I finished college instead of joining my fiancé to travel with the Christian music group with which he toured like we really wanted to do. As a teacher, I was patient with students who were impatient to learn to read all of the words in beautifully illustrated books and write down all of their thoughts in ways that others understand without question. As a wife and a mom, I must rely on patience to maintain a peaceful home atmosphere and allow even disagreements to become teachable moments for my family.

But I am not always good at being patient. We live in an instant-gratification society of fast food, microwave meals, texting, high-speed Internet, and Google. You don't even have to take the time to type out questions on the computer these days to get the answers you desire. Instead, you can simply use your voice to speak to your smart phone or home's electronic personal assistant and get the answer read back to you. There are times when I want what I want, and I want it right away; times when I feel too tired to keep being patient with the drivers around me or even my own children discussing a difference in opinion.

Galatians 5:22-23 speaks to patience, "But the fruit of the Spirit is love, joy, peace, patience, gentleness, goodness, faith, meekness, and self-control; against such there is no law" (MEV). The Amplified Bible expounds on patience in verse 23 of Galatians chapter 5 stating that it is "not the ability to wait, but how we act while waiting." Ouch!

Waiting is a natural part of life. We have no choice, oftentimes, but to wait. We sometimes have to wait in lines at the amusement park, wait to be seated in a restaurant, wait for the light to turn green, wait for the car to back out of the space in which we plan to park, wait for test results to come back, wait for that life-changing call to come, wait for our loved one to return home. How we act while we are waiting, however, is a choice we must make, and is reflective of our character. What thoughts do we allow to remain in our minds as we ruminate on the situation we face? Do our facial expressions and body language reflect a patient, Christ-like attitude? Are the fruits of the Spirit evident in our behaviors? People are watching us. What do they see?

Our Thoughts

Scripture admonishes us to take our thoughts captive (2 Corinthians 10:5, MEV), so clearly, we have control over what we allow to be the focus of our attention. It might not be an easy task, however. Sometimes when things around us are difficult and we feel weak or overwhelmed with life, it is easy for us to wallow in self-pity and disconnect from those who love us - even from our Heavenly Father! But when we make a conscious choice to control our thoughts, set a Godly example in our behaviors, and wait patiently on something to happen, something inevitably happens in our own development.

Isaiah writes, "But those who wait upon the Lord shall renew their strength; they shall mount up with wings as eagles, they shall run and not be weary, and they shall walk and not faint" (Isaiah 40:31, MEV). The Holman Christian Standard Bible uses the word "trust" in place of "wait" and the New International Version uses the word "hope." The Amplified version of this same verse reads, "But those who wait for the Lord [who expect, look for, and hope in Him] will gain new strength *and* renew their power; They will lift up their wings [and rise up close to God] like eagles [rising toward the sun]; They will run and not become weary, they will walk and not grow tired" (Isaiah 40:31, AMP). What a source of encouragement that is in times of waiting!

As we wait, control our thoughts to think on His words, and trust and hope in Him, He will strengthen us to run the race that is ours. Sometimes we have a tendency to think that waiting is a waste of time. It isn't. God has something good for us, even when we are waiting. We were in a season of waiting. We were waiting for healing to be evident in our son.

Sometimes we think that waiting is a waste of time. It isn't. God has something good for us, even when we are waiting.

He Knows Our Need

We lived an hour away from the hospital and clinic, and it was quickly learned that an hour was too far away to live. Caleb was dealing with a good bit of nausea, and he was very weak. The treatments Caleb would be undergoing included week-long stays in the hospital followed by 3-4 days of traveling an hour back and forth to the oncology clinic for tests, scans, chemotherapy, check-ups - all repeated for several months. This was of huge concern to Keith and me, but we had not talked to anyone else about it. Our health insurance coverage was through my work, so Keith was the one who had to quit working to care for Caleb. Down to just my income and the additional expenses that came with treatment, there was no way that we could afford to rent something closer to town.

Keith and I were sitting in a waiting room discussing our housing options when Keith's phone rang. The display showed a number that neither of us recognized. Upon answering, Keith discovered it was a friend from church calling to check on Caleb and us. He also had another reason for calling.

He and his wife had been trying to sell their condo in town for a couple of years, and it had not yet sold. It was only about 15 minutes from the hospital. He offered it to us to live in for the duration of Caleb's treatment. We were completely overwhelmed by the timing and the generosity of this friend! Who gives you a house to live in?

Only God could have orchestrated the timing of this call. No one even knew that it was a concern to us. But God knew. While we waited, God was working the miraculous on our behalf, showing us that no need had escaped His attention or ability to handle it. We didn't have to worry. His timing is perfect – even to the very moment the call was received. It was as though the Lord was saying, I know every single need you have the very moment it is on your heart and before it escapes your lips. I will provide for every need just like I say I will in my Word. "And my God will supply every need of yours according to His riches in glory in Christ Jesus" (Philippians 4:19, ESV).

Keith expressed our appreciation to our friend and told him we would let him know after we had talked and prayed about it. Keith and I shared about the offer with his parents, and they immediately offered to let us move in with them as well. They lived just under twenty minutes away from the hospital, and as his mom was retired, she offered to help watch after Joshua as well when Keith was with Caleb and I was at work. Keith and I prayed about it and decided that would be a better arrangement for our family. Their house was large enough to allow the boys to share a room and for Keith and me to share a room directly beside them. We packed most of our clothes and a few of our favorite things and moved from a three-bedroom home into two bedrooms.

The Move

It would not be easy. I love my in-laws. I always have. They are funny, they are kind, they absolutely spoil my children, and they are generous with their love for us. But Keith and I had been on our own for a long time. Moving in with parents had never been something we thought we would ever need do. We would not have the same privacy as a couple or as a family that we'd relished for the past fifteen years. But God, who knew that we would need their loving care and support, used them to provide what we needed, and He also gave all of us the grace to adapt to the changes. God's grace and timing are miraculous.

So we were very close to the hospital. That was such a blessing and made the traveling back and forth for Keith and Caleb so much easier and infinitely more cost effective. The only problem was that my job was now almost an hour away.

This did not surprise God in the slightest. His plans for us are perfect. Perfect! That means completely, 100 percent without fault, and thoroughly flawless. God had a perfect plan – a solution for the problem of my job being an hour away as a result of the move. One of my dearest friends from work - the school that was almost an hour away from where I now resided - lived about five minutes from Keith's parents. She offered to allow me to carpool back and forth to work with her every day. We could alternate weeks driving, thus saving both of us money.

I can tell you that this was more of a blessing to me than she could have possibly known. The two hours a day commuting with this precious friend was filled with times of faith-building encouragement for both of us. She made this time preciously productive for me. There was absolutely nothing I wanted more, other than his healing, than being with Caleb every moment that he endured the difficult journey he faced. But the words my friend spoke daily were full of life and hope. Even the drive time, waiting to get to work, the wait - gave me the strength that I needed each day.

God is Moving

There are times when God is working in our lives and we are unaware of the intricacies of His moving. There are other times when, if we are paying attention, we can see glimpses of Him working miracles on our behalf. God moves in His perfect timing, and we were looking for miracles - because we were desperate for them. He did not disappoint.

Many times we're unaware of the intricacies of God moving, but if we're intentional, we can see glimpses of miracles on our behalf.

One way in which God moves miraculously is when He uses others to communicate His encouragement to us. My friend did this daily on our drive back and forth to work. Others were also a source of miraculous encouragement. Keith was determined to be a rock for our family. I hardly ever saw him fall apart in weakness. We made a good team in this regard - times when I was melting under the stress of the news I heard from doctors and even from well-meaning people who knew someone who'd had cancer before - he never faltered when I needed him to be strong for me. On the rare occasion when his faith seemed weak, God's grace enabled me to have the right words to say to strengthen him - reminding him of how we had already seen God move and the promises in Scripture on which we were standing.

God wants to speak to us in whatever way that we will listen. He may speak in times of prayer, when reading the Word, during times of worship, through His Spirit in that still, small voice. He might speak through dreams and visions, and whatever other creative way that He chooses. His timing is always perfect; His desire is for relationship with us, and you cannot truly have a relationship without communication. It often amazed us the lengths that the Lord would go in order to communicate His love to us.

God wants to speak to us
in whatever way that we will listen.

God often used other people to communicate His love to us; reminding us that He was not going to allow us to walk this journey alone. Keith received three messages from three different people, in three different, private formats. It happened all within a period of 24 hours – the repetition could not be missed. Not one person knew the other person had sent him a message.

The first message he received stated that during a time of prayer, they felt prompted to share with Keith that God was his rock. He saw us standing on a huge rock with waves crashing around us, but we remained firm on the rock. He encouraged us to stand on God, Who is the rock of our salvation. Another text received referenced a song this person had on her heart for us that particular day. It was an excerpt from an old hymn remade by Hillsong Church, "You are the Rock on which I stand, by Your grace it is well. My hope is sure in Christ my Savior. It is well with my soul" (2011). The third message was sent by email and the sender told Keith that he had been praying specifically that Keith would be the rock for his family while he stood on the Rock. He said that he knew that Jesus was the Rock and that he didn't normally speak such bold words to others, but he felt it would be significant to Keith. Each person had referenced God being our rock and Keith received the messages over a two-day period.

God was definitely speaking to us through His children and reminding us that He would be our strength as we stood in faith on Christ the Rock. He knew that we would need reminders of His love and power to keep our faith grounded in His Truths. He continued to make His supernatural love for us known over and over again, in His timing – and whenever He knew we needed it.

The Supernatural

Webster defines supernatural as, "unable to be explained by science or the laws of nature" (Merriam-Webster, 2015). As we believe in an all-knowing, all-powerful God, we certainly believe in the supernatural. We know that God can and does move among His people in a multitude of ways, but my exposure to His moving power was a bit limited. Keith, likewise, had never had his eyes open to seeing much of the supernatural.

But just because you cannot see a thing does not make it any less real. One afternoon, Keith and Caleb were praying and talking about angels and the fact that angels were all around them, and Keith saw a huge angel standing in front of Caleb's door. It was a vision that lasted just a split second - one of those things that make you just stare, almost in disbelief, yet knowing what you saw. Keith described it to me later as a mist - there one moment and gone the next. Keith asked Caleb if he had seen anything, and Caleb said he saw a flash of something but he wasn't sure what it was.

Just a couple of days after Keith had seen the angel who appeared to be protecting our son – standing at the door of Caleb's room, we were at church for warm-up with the choir and band. The beginning of this Sunday morning was no exception to our familiar routine, but we soon experienced something extra special. Caleb was walking from the choir room into the sanctuary. When he neared the platform, he saw about 25 angels lined up across the altar shoulder to shoulder with blazing swords. He said he saw it only a moment, but immediately shared his vision with his dad.

Moments later, I walked from the choir room into the sanctuary when one of the ladies from the church stopped me. To tell you something of her, she is a woman of great diligence in prayer. She is highly respected among all who know her or know of her, and I consider her someone trustworthy to receive confidential prayer requests. I believe that not only does she spend a great deal of time in prayer over needs given to her, but also that God speaks to her. She approached me this Sunday morning and told me that she had been praying over Caleb. As she prayed, she said that she saw a vision of Caleb surrounded by angels, ready to fight on his behalf. Neither this woman nor I knew of Caleb's vision moments earlier, and he did not know of the vision God had given her, either.

All of this confirmed to us that not only was God on our side, but He was fighting this battle for us. The battle was the Lord's. As it is written in 1 Samuel 17:47, "And everyone assembled here will know that the Lord rescues His people, but not with sword and spear. This is the Lord's battle, and He will give you to us!" (NLT). This verse is an excerpt from the story of David and Goliath. Before David flings the first stone, he declares to Goliath that he comes to battle in the name of the "Lord of Heaven's armies" (1 Samuel 27:45, NLT).

We were undeniably in a battle, but we were not fighting alone. In any battle you are facing, you can know with confidence (in faith!) that you, as a child of God, are not alone, either. Even Paul, in the New Testament, writes, "What shall we say about such wonderful things as these? If God is for us, who can ever be against us?" (Romans 8:31, NLT). Likewise, Hebrews 13:5b-6a reads, "For God has said, 'I will never fail you. I will never abandon you.' So we can say with confidence, 'The Lord is my helper, so I will have no fear.'" (NLT).

As a mama, that excited me. Scripture tells us clearly that there are angels assigned to us. Matthew 18:10 reads, "Beware that you don't look down on any of these little ones (children). For I tell you that in Heaven, their angels are always in the presence of my heavenly Father" (NLT). And that was Jesus speaking! Another encouraging Scripture found in Hebrews reads, "Are not all the angels ministering spirits sent out [by God] to serve (accompany, protect) those who will inherit salvation? [Of course they are!]" (Hebrews 1:14, AMP).

To know that there are specific angels in charge of Caleb for his protection who are in the presence of God the Father to get instructions on what to do on Caleb's behalf is very exciting. But that should be just as exciting for you because the same applies to each one of us! Keith had seen an angel, Caleb had seen a multitude of warring angels, and this dear saint of God had seen a vision of the same surrounding my son. That is an assuring thought indeed, but knowing that God loved us enough to allow us a glimpse of these magnificent and powerful beings and then provided confirmation of the same on multiple occasions to help us know we weren't just imagining it - that is nothing short of amazing, and His timing was perfect.

Trusting in the Wait

Now we just waited for healing to be evident, trusting that God would move in His timing. He was showing us that He would be with us every step. We knew that Caleb was not a sick boy trying to be healed, but the healed from whom the enemy was trying to steal health and wholeness (reference John 10:10). We had several Scriptures written down to confirm this truth as well. Isaiah 53:4-5 reads, "Yet it was our weaknesses He carried; it was our sorrows (sicknesses) that weighed him down. And we thought His troubles were a punishment from God, a punishment for His own sins! But He was pierced for our rebellion, crushed for our sins. He was beaten so we could be whole. He was whipped so we could be healed" (NLT). On the same topic, 1 Peter 2:24 reads, "He personally carried our sins in his body on the cross so that we can be dead to sin and live for what is right. By His wounds you *are* healed" (NLT, emphasis mine). This knowledge brought feelings of peace, though that didn't make the journey easy. There were many attacks, and Keith and I were not the only ones who fought them.

Questions

Caleb would at times journal about what he was going through, and he talked with us both often. He had questions. He wondered why this was happening to him and what he had done to deserve it. Perhaps these are questions you have even asked about difficult situations in which you have found yourself. Clearly, we didn't have all the answers to every question he asked. We did know that he had done nothing to deserve cancer, and often encouraged him with Scripture to keep his thoughts on the right track.

One evening, when Caleb could not sleep, he lay down with Keith just to talk. Keith spoke hope to him, reminding him that God had a plan for his life (reference Jeremiah 29:11) and that there was a purpose for the gifts God had planted in his life. God's purpose for Caleb was not for him to die at 11 or 12 without fulfilling his calling. Keith shared Scripture from Psalms to encourage him, "I will not die; instead, I will live to tell what the Lord has done" (Psalm 118:17, NLT).

Death was often a topic that weighed heavily on the mind of my eleven-year-old son, and one that most children never even consider giving thought. Keith felt strongly that the Lord was going to use this battle as a part of Caleb's testimony. Furthermore, Keith believed that God had a powerful ministry in mind for Caleb's future. My prayers for a musical gifting in my son had not gone unanswered, and we believed that the remaining parts of that same prayer, that his musical gift would be used in ministry, would also be answered. God doesn't do things halfway. Keith prophesied to Caleb that he believed God would raise him from this sickness and that Caleb would have a supernatural anointing on his life when he played his music. He believed people would be healed by the power of God being ministered through Caleb, and that Caleb would touch the world with his gift, his testimony, and the powerful anointing on his life.

Keith had personally experienced God moving on listeners when he played his saxophone, and he believed that same anointing, and even more so, would be on our son. He believed Caleb would see miracles happen before his very eyes, and he told him so. These words refocused Caleb's mind, and he smiled as he drifted off to sleep.

Hope

Some may think that giving false hope is a terrible thing to do. In some ways, I agree. If you know that someone has no talent for singing because you have heard him or her sing, you might encourage that person to find a different area in the church to serve that is more suited to their unique gifts. Perhaps being a church greeter for someone with a bubbly personality would be a good match. In Caleb's situation, however, this was not false hope. Scripture backed us up, and we felt confident expectation that the Lord would not partially answer our prayer. Philippians 1:6 reads, "Being confident of this, that He who began a good work in you will carry it on to completion until the day of Christ Jesus" (NIV).

You can have confident expectation that the Lord will not partially answer prayer when you pray according to His Word.

Having hope in difficult situations is critical for a positive outlook and for a positive outcome. Pastor Bill Johnson (2015) taught about Biblical hope in a sermon to a congregation in the Netherlands:

"I think what makes us effective in this moment is that we are a people possessed by hope. Biblical hope is not a wish. The word hope in the Bible actually means the joyful anticipation of good. It is children on Christmas morning before they open presents. They can hardly contain themselves. If there is anything I could pray for us as believers, it would be for us to be possessed with Biblical hope, because that hope outlasts every bit of opposition."

Directing Caleb to think positively and offering Scripture to anchor his hopes was sound doctrinally. We wanted to give him every opportunity to believe that we could take God at His word and that hope would obliterate anything negative he thought. Philippians 4:8 admonishes us, "And now, dear brothers and sisters, one final thing. Fix your thoughts on what is true, and honorable, and right, and pure, and lovely, and admirable. Think about things that are excellent and worthy of praise" (NLT). We had to keep our thoughts, and help Caleb to keep his thoughts on positive things – joyfully anticipating God keeping His word.

Believe that you can take God at His word and know that Biblical hope will obliterate any negative thought.

Setting Anchor

If you are familiar with boating at all, you are aware that setting anchor, or putting the anchor that is attached to your boat into the water, helps keep your boat from drifting aimlessly across the water by digging into the bottom. The type of anchor you use depends on the type of ground below you. According to the Captain Shel Miller, true wind is described as the wind that blows across water or land. Apparent wind, however, he defines as "the wind that is generated by our movement in combination with the true wind. The only time there is no apparent wind is when we are at rest and only feeling the effects of the true wind" (Miller, 2013).

God's Word overflows with promises that give us confident expectation - setting an anchor of hope. These prophetic words Keith spoke over Caleb and the encouragement he received coupled with Scripture offered a double anchor to keep his mind and emotions from being tossed to and fro with the apparent winds of the storm and attacks he faced. It kept him grounded, instead, on truth. They allowed him to be at rest as he was anchored to the truth and hope found in the Word of God. That hope was something onto which He could hold. Hebrews 6:19a reads, "This hope is a strong and trustworthy anchor for our souls" (NLT). You can hold to hope despite apparent wind when you are firmly anchored in His truths and trust in God's timing.

God's Word overflows with promises that give us confident expectation setting an anchor of hope. Hold to hope.

5

Shining Brightly

Here's another way to put it: You're here to be light, bringing out the God-colors in the world. God is not a secret to be kept. We're going public with this, as public as a city on a hill. If I make you light-bearers, you don't think I'm going to hide you under a bucket, do you? I'm putting you on a light stand. Now that I've put you there on a hilltop, on a light stand – shine! Keep open house; be generous with your lives. By opening up to others, you'll prompt people to open up with God, this generous Father in heaven.
Matthew 5:14-16 (MSG)

We held to Biblical hope with tenacity. We were careful with our words. We worshiped. We listened for God to speak. We had our eyes open for every sign of His moving. God showed up time and again - speaking to us through others, through visions, through His Word, and we stayed encouraged every way in which we knew how.

Even after Caleb's first night of chemotherapy, the oncologist noted a difference in the feel of the tumor. Keith's response was that he couldn't wait until the oncologist came back and said she couldn't feel the tumor at all! Staying focused on hope and staying in the Word of God not only impacted us, but also affected our situation.

The Lord was faithful to be found every time He was sought. Scripture tells us, "Be strong and of a good courage. Fear not, nor be afraid of them, for the Lord your God, it is He who goes with you. He will not fail you, nor forsake you" (Deuteronomy 31:6, MEV). Likewise, James 4:8 says, "Draw near to God, and He will draw near to you" (MEV). He does not hide Himself from us, playing hard-to-get. Having a relationship with Jesus isn't like a game of hide-and-seek. Our pastor has recently said that God doesn't hide things from us, He hides them for us. He wants to be found.

We could feel the Lord bolstering our courage as we warred the enemy for our son. There were other children in the church who had recently been diagnosed with disease, and there was a general feeling of holy anger at the enemy for attacking these precious ones. We were determined to fight for them all and come against all manner of disease as the Lord brought it to mind.

The Lord is faithful to be found, every time He is sought.
Relationship with Jesus isn't a game of hide-and-seek.

The more we studied the Word of God and read about supernatural healing, the stronger our faith seemed to grow.

We read as much as we could on the topic and searched through the Bible and other available Christian resources to help us get a greater understanding of the truths of God's Word and the fact that He does indeed still perform miracles of many kinds. Keith looked up many verses in the Bible that promised healing and printed them out on index cards. We posted them all around the house so that we could see them and read them. I believe it takes a degree of courage to stand and blatantly tell people that you believe for miracles - to tell complete strangers of how God is working the miraculous on your behalf when you don't yet have physical proof to back you up.

Living in the Real World

We live in the natural world. While the supernatural (God moving) does often occur, not everyone is aware of it. There are other words some people use to describe these events (or similar events) and the people who believe in them - words like weird, freaky, luck, chance, abnormal, bizarre, peculiar, unusual. But God will give you the grace (the power) to have a Godly confidence and boldness to stand in faith despite what your natural senses are telling you. He will give you the grace to be a courageous believer.

God doesn't expect you to perform the miracle all by yourself. He does the work, or provides you the wisdom to use the gifts He has already placed in your hands. Sometimes He uses the gifts He has provided to others to bring forth miracles. We are called to put on gear to protect ourselves from attacks, and to fight the enemy with the Word of God. Believers are called to believe that God will do the work and then to stand firmly in that belief. Ephesians 6:13 reads, "Therefore take up the whole armor of God that you may be able to resist in the evil day, and having done all, to stand" (MEV). In other words, do all you can. Once you've done that, stand firmly. Believe.

God will give you the grace to have
a Godly confidence and boldness to stand in faith
despite what your natural senses are telling you.

Exercise

Pastor Bill Johnson (2015) prayed for God's people to have "supernatural courage. Courage beyond our personalities. Courage beyond our natural giftings." When you exercise a muscle often enough, it begins to grow stronger and you can take on more weight. We exercised our faith muscle every single day, and our faith grew stronger. It was our priority, and there were days we felt so strong that we believed we would see many miracles occur. It was an unshakable faith, a holy boldness, and we could visualize no other outcome than complete healing for Caleb and for those for whom we prayed.

Our physical bodies need exercise to conquer the flab, help control weight, build strength and endurance, and a multitude of other health benefits. I don't go to the gym like I should, though I do have a membership card at the YMCA. I know it is something I should do, something that I need to do. I come up with excuses - I'm too busy, I'm too tired, I didn't get up when the alarm clock sounded, or perhaps I forgot to set my alarm. I have heard it said that the most difficult part of exercising is opening the gym door. For me, it seems to be harder to walk out of my own front door.

I haven't made exercise a priority in my life. But when I go, I don't concern myself with how I look doing the exercises. I am there with a goal in mind - to work my muscles and get my blood pumping. What I look like when I am exercising doesn't matter to me when I am focused on my goal. The motions I am making and the effort I am putting forth are moving me toward a healthy objective I have set.

Your spirit man also needs exercise. I'm so thankful that I didn't make excuses for why I couldn't exercise my faith. If I had, I might not have had the same outcome. Exert your faith muscle with the repetition of God's truths and you will build the courage needed to conquer your opponent - the devil. Come against him with the Word of God and Scripture assures us that he must flee.

Spiritual weakness is something you can't afford, even more so than physical weakness. And it isn't something you have to wait until you are in a crisis to decide to do. One of the easiest times to exercise is when you are already in fairly good shape. But regardless of the difficulty level, no matter where you are on life's journey, the best thing that you can do when you need to exercise is to start. You can find your strength in Him, and you don't even have to leave your house daily to do it.

Exercise your faith muscle with the repetition of God's truths and you will build the courage needed to conquer your opponent.

It is amazing to me how God will help you as you study the Bible. He is like your very own personal trainer! It is His desire to have relationship with us, and He won't hold Himself apart in hiding from those who seek Him. In our case, it was like God was sending Scripture to us that we could use in the battle in which we found ourselves.

I will say it again, having a relationship with God isn't like a game of hide-and-seek. He desires to be found by you! Jesus said in Luke 11:9, "And so I tell you, keep on asking, and you will receive what you ask for. Keep on seeking, and you will find. Keep on knocking, and the door will be open to you." (NLT)

God won't hold Himself apart in hiding from those who seek Him.

We are God's Masterpiece

Keith and I both receive some of our devotionals through electronic mail. One of the e-mails that Keith received was focused on Ephesians 2:1-13, and he found a beautiful golden nugget right in the middle of that passage in verse 10, "For we are God's masterpiece. He has created us anew in Christ Jesus, so we can do the good things He planned for us long ago" (NLT).

He read that verse and then began to pray with thanksgiving that Caleb was God's masterpiece. God made Caleb and gave him some specific and amazing gifts, and His Word said that God had good things planned for Caleb. He thanked God again and told Him that he was trusting God to create Caleb anew and make him whole as God had said He would do so that Caleb could do those good things to the glory of God. Keith knew God had a plan for Caleb, and thanked our Father again for His goodness and love toward our son. He thanked God for shining a light brightly on that truth from His Word, and he applied the Word of God to our specific situation.

James 5:16 states, "The effective, fervent prayer of a righteous man accomplishes much" (MEV). There is a lot of hope in that verse, and it is one of my favorites. There's probably nothing I dislike more than wasting my time. I love that God's Word tells me that the time I spend praying is effective and not a waste of my time.

But what exactly is fervent prayer? How do you know if you are being fervent enough? One of my favorite Bible teachers, Jack Hayford, explains this kind of fervency in prayer. Describing "fervency" he wrote, "Energeo describes a process that is far more than energetic. Energeo accomplishes its goal" (Hayford, 2015b).

Pastor Hayford (2015b) continues by describing that fervency in prayer "is not based in pointless emotionalism. It is a passion in prayer that is confident of certain fulfillment. It is based upon the surety of God's partnership in bringing His kingdom rule into our world as we pray." Our prayers accomplish much, accomplishes the goal, not from necessarily wailing and crying in desperation, but because of a confident faith that God will fulfill what we are asking Him to do! Now that confident faith may sound like loud wailing, it may look like crying or kneeling, or lying prostrate on the floor, but it is the faith or belief behind the words, not the position of the body that makes the prayer passionate. You don't have to be loud, because God isn't deaf. But as our pastor often said, He also isn't nervous! However, you need to pray until you feel you have "prayed through" or prayed all that you need to pray at the time – just communicate with Him!

God is Faithful to His Word

Isaiah 55:11 states that God's Word would not return to Him without accomplishing what He sent it to do. That is the reason why we pray His Word back to Him. I like to pray it aloud. Then not only does He hear it, but we hear it as well. Scripture even says, "So then faith comes by hearing, and hearing by the Word of God" (Romans 10:17, MEV). Or, faith comes by hearing the Word of God. So as you are reading Scripture aloud, you see the Word, you speak the Word (returning it to Him), and you hear the Word, which simultaneously builds your faith.

In the natural, probably the one voice you will always believe is your own. So there is something to be said for hearing yourself say something. As we know that we consider ourselves truthful beings, especially as we are focusing on seeking or speaking the truth of the Word of God, we find it easier to believe what we say aloud ourselves.

Have you ever listened to someone tell a story and wonder if it really happened that way? But if you have lived something yourself or seen it for yourself and tell a friend honestly about your experience, you don't doubt what you say. You can't doubt what you have lived. A person can even talk themselves into or out of doing something. Our words are indeed very powerful.

You can't doubt what you've lived.

Scripture says, "It is not the flesh that gives a person life. It is the spirit that gives life. The *words* I told you are spirit, and so they give life" (John 6:63, ICB, emphasis mine). The reference here to the *word* that is spoken is "rhema" from the original Greek word "rheo" which is a verb that means to utter. Rhema is a noun defined "that which is or has been uttered by the living voice" (Bible Study Tools, 2014).

Rhema can be God speaking to you, revealing truths in His Word as it applies to you right now. The Holy Spirit speaks these words of life to you, instilling in you hope and understanding as it applies to you then. It is because God's Word is living that one verse may mean one thing to you in one season of your life yet may speak to you in a totally different way with a different meaning at a later season in life. It is the Holy Spirit speaking to you and making God's Word come alive to you.

All of this works together in prayer. The Holy Spirit reveals truths to you and makes Scripture come alive. This stirs your faith and gives you a boldness to pray the Word fervently, resulting in building an even stronger faith and also returning God's Word to Him. It all works so beautifully together, and only our loving Father could have put it together so.

Schedules and Craziness

Caleb seemed to adjust to the chemotherapy schedule as well as I could possibly imagine. He kept a positive attitude overall. He was never snippy with the nurses or doctors, and never wanted to be a bother to anyone. Chemotherapy, once begun, keeps a very precise schedule. They test blood count, check urine level; all of the numbers have to be perfect in order to administer the potent medicines that are scheduled.

The first week the nurses couldn't get his fluids and numbers leveled off until it was quite late in the evening, so chemo didn't begin until 10 PM. Therefore, that would be his nightly routine that week, with chemotherapy beginning at 10:00 each night for five nights. After the completion of the medicines one night during the first week, the nurses administered a drug through his port that would allow him to relax and sleep.

He had a severe reaction to the medicine in the form of hallucinations. He was seeing people standing all around him, and he saw skulls flying out of his bed. He thought his bed was a ship that was hovering in the air and that the IV bags hanging from the IV poles were frightening fish with big teeth flying around and swooping down trying to attack him. He kept trying to get out of his bed, which of course we could not let him do because of all of the tubes going into his chest through the port. He was completely freaking out, waving his arms everywhere and thrashing around his bed.

We called his nurse, who quickly came but said there was nothing she could do. They couldn't give him anything to offset the side effects; we would just have to wait until the medicine wore off. I climbed into the bed with him, and used my arms and legs to help hold him in the bed. I talked to him, tried to rationalize with him using the truth of reality to try to combat the effects of the medicine, but that was not working.

I was in tears, and began crying out to the Lord for help, praying for wisdom to know what to do.

Keith pulled out his phone and put on some worship music by the Christian group Planetshakers, and Caleb immediately began to calm down. He was lying on his back and suddenly he lifted his hands and started crying out to God to help him and to be with him. He told God that he really needed Him. The whole atmosphere in the room changed as Caleb began to worship our heavenly Father. It was so moving as parents, watching our son crying out to God for himself. He did so without the prompting of his mom and dad or just relying on his parents' faith. In minutes, Caleb fell asleep. God is so faithful to turn something so dreadful into a beautiful time of peace.

Later that morning, two women from the psychiatry department came to speak with Keith and Caleb. I am certain this is part of the protocol offered to families who have life-threatening illnesses, to make sure that everyone is okay and adjusting as well as possible to the changes going on in their lives. One of the ladies was asking Caleb about what fears he had. She rambled on and on about fear. She kept talking about death and the high chance he had of dying. She wanted to know if he ever felt scared of dying. Caleb responded that he wasn't afraid of that at all. She asked him why he wasn't afraid of dying, and Caleb said that God had told him earlier that day that he was going to be okay.

The psychiatrist asked, "You hear voices sometimes?"

Caleb responded, “Yes ma’am.”

“What do the voices tell you?” she asked.

“God told me that I was going to be alright.” Caleb responded.

“Was that your inner voice talking to you?” she inquired.

“No ma’am.”

“Did you hear it from the outside, through your ears?”

“No ma’am.”

“If it wasn’t your inner voice, and you didn’t hear it from the outside, what do you think it was?” she probed.

Caleb responded, “It wasn’t my inner voice. It was God speaking to me.”

“Okay.”

I don’t know what this lady wrote down in her notebook about my son, but I love that Caleb was confident in what he knew to be truth. I’m thankful that God loves us enough to communicate to us all, no matter our age. He doesn’t hold Himself apart and speak only to those who devote hours upon hours of study in His Word. He doesn’t hold back from all except those who have completed seminary, or have achieved other proofs of high intelligence or religious training. First Corinthians 2:14 reads, “But the natural man does not receive the things of the Spirit of God, for they are foolishness to him; nor can he know them, because they are spiritually discerned” (MEV).

When the women left, Keith and Caleb prayed for them. They prayed that they would be drawn to relationship with God and that *they* would hear His voice and believe. Caleb wanted to know why they were asking him so many questions and focusing so much on death. Keith shared the Scripture from 1 Corinthians with Caleb and explained it in a way that he could understand it. It is when a person seeks the Lord and begins to spend time with the Lord in His Word and in prayer that they begin to recognize Him speaking into their life.

Recognition

The more you get to know someone, the more likely you are to recognize their voice. When you spend a lot of time with someone, you can even hear them calling you in a crowd. It is like that with God as well. The more time you spend with Him, developing a relationship with Him, the more familiar you are with His character and can distinguish His voice from the other noises that clamor for our attention. It is even easier to do this when you are aware that He is ever-present and desiring to communicate with you.

The more you know someone,
the more likely you are to recognize their voice
above the din and distractions of life.

While it is a little humorous thinking on the shocked, wide-eyed looks the faces of the psychiatrists held as they listened to this young child explain the Voice he heard that kept fear of the medical reality at bay, it is also a bit sad that they hadn't experienced the drawing of the Lord for themselves. Keith and Caleb prayed that the words shared would plant a seed in their hearts as they heard Caleb's witness of a loving Father Who cares about our own emotions. How grateful I am that I know my Savior's voice! What a privilege that He desires to communicate with His people! He doesn't hold Himself aloof, and we can't hide from His love for us. He loves each of us so much that He gave His Son, Jesus, as a sacrifice for us so that we could have an eternity with Him (John 3:16, paraphrased).

Caleb continued the week of chemotherapy, though the drug that had caused the hallucinations was added to a list of allergies on his chart. I was thankful that type of night would not be repeated. The nurses offered Tylenol to ease pain at night after the chemotherapy was completed. One night Caleb couldn't sleep even after he had received Tylenol. He thought Benadryl might help him sleep, but I put on some music by Hillsong and turned off the lights. He was asleep in no time. No Benadryl, no anxiety attacks. I was very thankful. God is so faithful.

Surrounded by Truth

The doctors continued to examine the tumor in Caleb's leg and noted that while it hadn't changed in size, they felt it softening. They were quite surprised that it had softened so much so quickly. We just smiled every time they said that and explained that with chemotherapy and prayer, that tumor was going away. We brought index cards with Bible verses about healing to the hospital room with us each time we were there. The doctors saw the index cards labeled with Scripture decorating many surfaces about the room. Poster Putty is such an awesome resource for that!

We were surrounded by the Truth of the promises of God. Scripture tells us, "For every one of God's promises is 'Yes' in Him. Therefore, the 'Amen' is also spoken through Him by us for God's glory" (2 Corinthians 1:20, HCSB). The Amplified version of this same verse explains it further, reading, "For as many as are the promises of God, in Christ they are [all answered] 'Yes.' So through Him we say our 'Amen' to the glory of God" (AMP). The Message translation puts this Scripture in even more common terminology. It reads, "Whatever God has promised gets stamped with the Yes of Jesus. In Him, this is what we preach and pray, the great Amen, God's Yes and our Yes together, gloriously evident. God affirms us, making us a sure thing in Christ, putting His Yes within us. By His Spirit He has stamped us with His eternal pledge - a sure beginning of what He is destined to complete" (2 Corinthians 1:20-22, MSG).

Drop the mic! Not only are God's promises true, but we get to partner with Him when we pray His Word. Furthermore, He makes sure that we don't end up looking like idiots in the long run. He "affirms us, making us a sure thing!" The coupling of God's "Yes!" and our "Yes!" categorically brings certainty, confidence, and courage in God's promises. We can trust that His Word will accomplish exactly what He said it would. Our speaking His promises aloud is just the beginning, and He is destined, predetermined, and compelled to bring the promise to pass. And we can say "Amen!" to that!

The coupling of God's "Yes!" and our "Yes!" categorically brings certainty, confidence, and courage in God's promises.

We prayed that each hospital staff member would be as impacted by the words of Truth posted as we were. The staff was such a blessing to us. The nurses tirelessly tended to our son all through the day, and always inquired if we needed anything ourselves each time they entered our room. The doctors were present each morning for rounds to check his progress as well and to see if we had questions. They were all good to us, and it would be impossible to physically repay them for their loving efforts. So we prayed for them, and prayed that God's love for them would shine brightly through the things that we said and did. We wanted to make a difference in them, just as they gave of themselves to us.

In the same way, let your good deeds shine out for all to see, so that everyone will praise your Heavenly Father.
Matthew 5:16 (NLT)

6

Thankfulness in Everything

Always by joyful. Never stop praying.
Be thankful in all circumstances,
for this is God's will for you who belong to Christ Jesus.
1 Thessalonians 5:16-18 (NLT)

Have you ever been on a vacation for several days? You love getting away. As long as you are gone, your focus is on the present activities, living in the moment, making memories. You don't think of every detail of things you are not seeing or doing at home. That is a portion of the appeal of vacationing. You leave the routine for a bit and aren't as concerned about all of the details of taking care of a household or making a living.

But when you get back home, you sometimes realize how much you have missed your routine or your own space. Taking a hot shower in your own bathroom and finally slipping comfortably under your own clean sheets often brings such a feeling that washes over all of you, from head to toe, as you sigh and relax against the plush comfort of your own mattress. There's just something about coming home that is especially sweet, no matter how much fun you've had while you have been away.

We were certainly not on any kind of vacation, but leaving home and moving in with my in-laws was not something I would have wanted to do under normal circumstances. Keith and I had been married and independent a long time. Don't get me wrong, I cannot tell you how thankful I was and still am for the way they lovingly cared for us. I could weep just thinking about their generosity and graciousness to us. It was a gift. It was the most beneficial thing for our family.

However, there were some drawbacks. I missed not having to be so terribly careful with every discussion. The normal privacy of our small family was missing. It was stressful trying to make certain the children kept their areas picked up, stayed quiet, and were aware of the other adults in the household. They don't love keeping things picked up, and don't feel the slightest pressure when things are not orderly. This was a big adjustment for them, and the pressure I felt, however self-imposed, was very real. Our life no longer was our familiar routine.

Our two dogs had to come with us, so there was that meshing of our pets with the pet of our in-laws. All that we had been used to was completely turned over. The kitchen was not mine, the pantry was not mine, and the washing machine and dryer were not mine. If I had taken the time to fully think through all that I was giving up with my little family, I could have really wallowed in self-pity. I even missed my houseplants. It's all the simple, day-to-day things I missed that we so often took for granted.

Even my boys were missing things. They missed the privacy of having their own bedrooms as well. They missed having a chest of drawers and closet of their own. Each child was given two drawers for his clothes, and they also shared a portion of a closet in their now-shared room. There was a plastic box that fit under the bed for toys they brought from home.

They felt weird knowing that they were one door away from their parents' room and two doors away from their grandparents' room. They felt the pressure of having to be quiet and not having all of their things with them. They missed the freedom of riding their four wheelers on our property and walking in the woods in the rural area where we lived. They missed having their dog sleep in the bed with them.

Joshua struggled with feeling like he was never going to get any attention of his own. Aware of all the attention surrounding Caleb, he felt overlooked since he was "just" a normal kid. He thrives on attention, so this came as quite a hit to his self-esteem. He later said that he often wondered if anyone cared about or noticed him at all.

He looked at the other children in the clinic and in the hospital. He saw their suffering. He met children, even younger than he and his brother, who were sick. He heard of children who battled the disease and died. He found the atmosphere depressing. Sickness and death are topics to which children generally do not give any thought. Climbing on the monkey bars, jumping from swings, and playing their electronic games are about as far as their minds generally travel. They don't typically consider even breaking an arm as a consequence to a poor landing on the playground.

I am certain that if my in-laws had taken the time to think of all they were giving up, they could have had a pity-party of their own. Their privacy was equally gone. The quiet, orderly home of a family who had already reared their children had also been turned upside down. There were more mouths to feed, two extra dogs with which to contend while I was at work and Keith was at the hospital or clinic, and a child who needed supervising, entertaining, and assisting with schoolwork.

If they had worries or concerns about the disruption of their own routine or the additional expenses, they never voiced it within our hearing. My mother-in-law kept things tidy, cooked meals for us, took care of our dogs, cared for Joshua and helped stay on top of his schooling, and made trips back and forth to the hospital and clinic. She made deviled eggs by the dozens, since they were Caleb's favorite and he had little appetite. No one complained. Every day when I arrived back at their house after work, dinner was always well in hand, with instructions to rest, or do whatever I needed to do. She took care of the household chores as she always had done, never allowing me to do more than keep our shared bathroom and rooms clean, and taking care of our own laundry. My in-laws deserve a gold star.

My parents helped to make sure that things at our house in the country was well cared for. They made many hour-long trips from their home or after work to visit us in the hospital, and were there to assist any time help was needed. Like my in-laws, they spent much time in prayer for each of us. There was so much to be thankful for every single day, and that was our focus. We were learning lessons on contentment and developing an appreciation of the little things we so often took for granted every day.

Tough Times

To say that it would have been easy to have had a different outlook is an understatement. Caleb, like his mama, despises needles. I used to joke that it was a miracle that I ever had more than one child since with every doctor appointment I got my finger stuck by a nurse who undoubtedly thought I was ridiculous. My palms are always clammy when I know I am getting a simple finger prick. I remember at the beginning of Caleb's journey a nurse was going to need to prick his finger for a test. We did everything short of spanking him to coerce him into being still enough for the nurse to do her job.

Frankly, as sympathetic as I was to his feelings, even I felt embarrassed by his behavior. At last still, she quickly jabbed his finger. He snatched it away causing the lancet to slice across his finger. No amount of talking could persuade Caleb to sit completely still and calm, and he paid a big price for jerking.

The purpose of the port that was put in his chest, just under the skin, was to allow the medicine to flow through a tube into a larger vein in his neck. But to access the port, the nurses had to stick him with a needle into his chest and then into the port. At the beginning of our journey, this was especially difficult for Caleb. Honestly, it was hard for us watching him. Caleb would grab two of my fingers and hold tightly, and the nurses would help us distract him. We soon also learned of a medicinal anesthetic cream to help numb the area before arriving.

After his first round of chemo, we were told that Caleb would need injections at home as well. I could feel a sense of panic coming. I sew, but injections . . . there was no way that I could do that to anyone, but especially not to my child. I am not a nurse. I have never had that kind of medical training! The nurses entered our room with saline, syringes, and a couple of oranges. We had a class in the hospital room on how to prepare and administer injections. I was absolutely terrified. After practicing on the orange several times, Keith volunteered to let me practice on him. I was freaking out. I told him that I could not do this, not to him, and not to Caleb. I just couldn't.

Let me just tell you – Keith is a very brave, patient, and persistent man. After much encouragement from the nurse and from Keith, I held my breath and thought of oranges as I injected Keith with saline. I didn't faint. I didn't throw up. Neither did Keith. We practiced several more times (never on myself), and the nurse felt we were ready to go pick up the medicine and use it on Caleb at home.

The First Injection

The first night home, we warmed the medicine using the body heat from our hands since it had to stay refrigerated until time to use. We thoroughly and carefully cleaned Caleb's little arm, and I watched as Keith administered the injection. We had not been told that the worst part came after the puncture. Caleb's arm started burning and he started crying. Keith and I felt terrible, inflicting this kind of pain on a child who was already suffering in ways no one ever should.

The pain of the medicine inside his leg began to subside after a few minutes and we were all able to calm down. I tossed the spent needle into the new container for storing used needles and looked at the remaining needles. He had to have one injection every single night for the next 6 days. I couldn't do this. I didn't know how Keith was going to be able to do this.

The Second Injection

The second night came. We had been dreading the injection all day long. We followed the preparations and had Caleb downstairs at my in-law's house. We were all there - Keith, me, Joshua, and Keith's family. It was our job to keep Caleb distracted so that Keith could quickly give him the injection. Caleb was not having it. He absolutely had a meltdown. Nothing we could do could convince him to be still, and it got to be a little bit frightening watching Keith wave that needle trying to locate the spot we had cleaned so carefully on a child who was crying with his mother trying desperately to keep him still.

I think that this was one of the worst nights of our whole journey. Everyone in that room was in tears. Keith's mom and I were both sobbing, Keith and I felt like horrible parents intentionally inflicting pain on our son. Joshua and Keith's stepdad were both distraught, and Caleb was in hysterics thrashing and crying, begging us not to do this to him. It was absolutely terrible.

Finally, realizing that it would be impossible for me to hold our son still, Keith handed me the needle, a fresh alcohol wipe, and the instructions that I would have to be the one to do it while he held Caleb down. My eyes nearly popped from their sockets. I couldn't do this. I had already said so! But nothing else would work. We had tried talking, bribing, reasoning, threatening, and physical restraint - and NOTHING else had worked.

Keith, a very big man in comparison to the eleven-year-old, laid on top of Caleb, effectively pinning him motionless on the family room floor. I hastily opened the wipe, scrubbed the back of his arm, and checked the medicine in the needle for air bubbles. Seeing none, and with the sounds of crying in the air, I quickly jabbed my boy's arm, pushed in the plunger, and removed the needle. I capped the syringe, tossed it in the disposal bin, and with my husband, held our crying son as he felt the burning of the medicine in his muscle. I think that is the most horrible and most necessary thing I have ever done to my son to date. And it was nothing like sticking an orange.

No Words to Say

As I mentioned earlier, Keith and I both try to be really careful about the things we say. We try to always incorporate Scripture when we pray, because since God's Word is always true we know that as long as we are praying His Word, we are praying the right thing. There are times in life, however, when you may not have time to quote a Scripture.

That night I did not have the presence of mind to think of a specific Scripture to give me the strength that I needed. God's Word is always true. But God doesn't have to wait for us to quote His Word for His Word to be in full effect. That night, Philippians 4:13 was fully in action even though it had not passed my lips. "For I can do everything through Christ, who gives me strength" (NLT). The King James Version reads, "I can do all things through Christ which strengtheneth me."

I once heard a pastor say, "in the Greek, ALL means all. In the Hebrew, ALL means all." Yes, ALL means all. Everything. There is NOTHING that I cannot do if God is with me. And His presence was definitely in the room enabling us to have the strength to do what we had to do for the benefit of our son.

God doesn't have to wait for us to quote His Word for His Word to be in full effect.

Help

We had a lengthy conversation the next morning with Caleb's oncologist. Knowing that we had five more days of injections to administer, we knew there had to be a better way. I don't know that we could have endured another night like the previous one. The doctor gave us several ideas to try. We also had a dear friend give us an idea to try, and the next night we put our new education to use. The solution she suggested was a simple one.

Ice. Put ice in a bag on the skin to numb the area before the injection. This became Caleb's personal nightly chore. He would place the ice on his leg while we prepped everything else, and when he said his leg was numb enough we would clean the area and administer the injection. Thank

God that we never had a repeat of that horrible night. Thank God the better way was found.

Years later, Caleb can handle an injection like it is nothing. I remember when he even quit using the anesthetic cream to numb the area before the nurses accessed his port. He told me that he was used to it. He would take a deep breath and they'd insert the needle and it would be over. I have even heard him comfort nurses who repeatedly missed the vein in his arm, telling them, "It's okay. It's okay." (Mama says it's not, though. Please get someone else!)

Thankfulness

Caleb was always so gracious to everyone who took care of him. We were thankful for the way we were cared for and encouraged, as well. God uses people to bring hope and encouragement to others, and we were recipients of this kind of love over and over again. Isaiah 61:1 (NLT) reads, "The Spirit of the Sovereign Lord is upon me, for the Lord has anointed me to bring good news to the poor. He has sent me to comfort the brokenhearted and to proclaim that captives will be freed."

I believe that we are all commissioned to bring the good news to others; to bring comfort to those who are hurting, just as Isaiah prophesied. And God doesn't just use people who are "pastors" to do this. If He is calling us to bring hope into an environment (and I believe that He calls us all to do this – to be salt and light to the world – reference Matthew 5:13-16), He will equip us to do that calling.

We are light bearers. We have the opportunity to impact those in our circle of influence, to act more like thermostats than thermometers as we set the atmosphere, not just respond to it. Scripture tells us, "If I make you light-bearers, you don't think I'm going to hide you under a bucket, do you? I'm putting you on a light stand. Now that I've put you there on a hilltop, on a light stand – shine! Keep open house; be generous with your lives. By opening up to others, you'll prompt people to open up with God, this generous Father in Heaven" (Matthew 5:15-16, MSG). And we are misguided if we believe that we can only make a difference if we do something really big, have a lot of money, or are very outgoing. In truth, anything that stops you from feeling like you can comfort or assist someone else is probably just a lie from the enemy to keep you from being a blessing to them.

Because God calls us to carry hope into oursurroundings, He will equip us to accomplish that calling.

Blessings upon Blessings

We had much for which to be thankful and there were so many people being generous with their lives for our benefit. We received countless hot meals delivered to our room at dinner time. We had visitors stop in to encourage us, pray with us, or just keep us up to date with events going on that we were not able to fully participate in because of the time spent caring for Caleb. People delivered other goodies to the hospital like coffee, cupcakes, or ice-cream. I cannot tell you how much these visits meant to our family at the time, what a difference it made on our outlook, and the lifelong impact it made on the idea that a seemingly miniscule act of kindness can truly make a tremendous difference in the life of a person.

These deliveries cost someone their time and money. The impact of that, however, was more than merely saving us the equal. It meant that we didn't have to determine how we were going to provide a meal when there was no kitchen for me to cook in at the hospital. It meant that our focus could just be on helping Caleb. It meant that we realized that we were not fighting this battle alone – that someone else cared enough to remember us and help provide for us. It meant that we didn't feel forgotten, but cherished.

It's the Simple Things

Perhaps you know someone who is in the hospital and you are wondering what you can do. You might wonder what you can say that will make a difference. You might think that the outlook is so bleak that nothing you can say or do will make a difference to them. But let me offer some insight and encouragement in this area. The idea that nothing you say or do in a situation you can't fix by yourself will matter is a lie from the enemy. You can make an impact, even if you don't hold a cure in your hand. In the years following Caleb's battle,

I can still remember many of the meals, texts, cards, and visits we received. We were immensely grateful. And while I cannot remember all of the conversations that were held or every word that was prayed over us in the many rooms we inhabited for what seemed like an eternity, I do remember that people loved us enough to pause from the busyness of their lives to demonstrate their love for us.

You can make an impact, even if you don't hold a cure in your hand. Sometimes people just need to know that they are loved and not forgotten.

I remember people coming and gathering around Caleb's hospital bed and praying for him. I remember receiving text messages from people asking if there was anything that we needed or wanted, or just letting us know that they were thinking about us and praying for us. I remember people coming and just sitting in the room with me so that there was another adult with whom to have conversation. I remember friends who whisked me off to dinner just to do something that had nothing to do with hospitals, sickness, or sadness. Let me tell you – these are all things that matter. And we were thankful. I have heard many times that people don't care how much you know until they know how much you care. I have found that to be true, and we were definitely feeling the compassion and care that others had for us.

Not one of those people ever told me that they knew exactly how I felt. They didn't and we knew that. Not one person told me they could fix Caleb or cause it all to stop. I never expected to hear those words from them because I knew my family and friends did not have this ability. The thing that we needed was to know that we were loved and not forgotten. It was important to hear that people were praying for us when I was so tired and didn't feel there was anything else I could pray at the moment.

I can remember moments of scrolling through Facebook and seeing life going on as normal for others. I remember that this sometimes created feelings of self-pity in myself. I could have wallowed in that, and the enemy would have delighted in that if I had. But even the simplest visit or text that prayers and thoughts were being sent Heavenward on our behalf ministered to us and chased symptoms of loneliness away. Never underestimate the impact of a kind word or deed on those who have a need – no matter the size of the need. I once heard the question, "How do you eat an elephant?" That sounds like an impossibility, but the answer was simple. "One bite at a time."

God Uses People

God was certainly using His people in big and small ways to make an indelible mark on our family. One November afternoon, Keith had posted on social media that Caleb wanted to sell (or trade) his Wii gaming system. He wanted to be able to purchase a Playstation3 with the proceeds. The Playstation3 had games more suitable for his age.

A friend called Keith that evening and said that he had seen Keith's post, and though he didn't have PlayStation3 to trade for Caleb's Wii, he was on his way to the store to purchase a gaming console and a couple of games and needed to know what kind of games Caleb would enjoy playing. Keith was absolutely stunned by this man's generosity. He explained to Keith how thankful he was that he had a healthy son and just wanted to give something to us that Caleb would really enjoy and would be a blessing to us. With a tight throat and tears in his eyes, Keith talked to him and thanked him profusely. The man said he would come to the hospital in just a little bit.

That evening, Keith, Joshua, and I were seated on the sofa talking to Caleb. He was hooked up to several IV bags and reclining on the bed covered by thin white sheets and a couple of freshly warmed hospital blankets. We heard a knock at the door over the sound of our conversation. Keith stood to open the door and a nurse was standing there with a gift bag in her hand. She said that someone had dropped the bag off for us.

Keith inquired of the nurse if the visitor had wanted to come in and she responded that they didn't – that it was their desire to remain anonymous. I darted out searching for our friend so that I could extend my appreciation, but saw no one that I recognized. When I returned to our room Caleb removed the fluffy white tissue paper from the large bag and excitedly removed a brand-new PlayStation3 console, controller, and games. He was ecstatic!

We watched with tear-filled eyes as he and Joshua excitedly talked back and forth about the surprise gift, and Keith picked up his phone to text our friend and express our gratitude. Just before he pressed "send" on the text, another knock sounded at the door. We exchanged a quick glance, and called for the visitor to come in to the room. The door opened, and there stood our friend with a brand-new PlayStation3 console under his arm and a rather full shopping bag in his hand. We just gaped at him as though he had three heads. I can only imagine what he was thinking as he stood there looking at Caleb sitting on the bed surrounded with treasures identical to what was under his arm! We were perplexed and Keith pointed at the game system next to Caleb and inquired of our friend, "This one isn't from you?"

We didn't know exactly what to do. We were definitely at a loss for words. We didn't want to say anything that would minimize in any way the generosity of this man and his family toward us, but we were bewilderingly processing what was going on! Our friend was a real champ, however, and gave us the receipt for everything that he had purchased for Caleb with the instructions to exchange it for whatever games Caleb would like to have or anything else that he would enjoy. After a brief visit, he left and Caleb returned to the first gift bag and noticed an enclosed card which was signed, "The Prayer Warriors."

To this day we have absolutely no idea who provided one of the extravagant gifts, but I can say that that night a couple of very excited boys were not thinking about needles and being stuck in a hospital room. We were very thankful. Isaiah 61:2b-3 points out some basic exchanges that are available to us, reading, "To comfort all who mourn, to preserve those who mourn in Zion, to give to them beauty for ashes, the oil of joy for mourning, the garment of praise for the spirit of heaviness, that they might be called trees of righteousness, the planting of the Lord, that He might be glorified" (MEV).

God had caused none of this destruction, anguish, sickness, dispiritedness, or life-altering changes we faced, but He already had a plan in place to turn each of our feelings around in a way that would bring Him glory. We had precious people who were praying for us and allowing God to use them to be a tremendous blessing during a very difficult time. I felt very thankful for their prayers, knowing they made an impact on our situation.

Give, and you will receive.
Your gift will return to you in full – pressed down, shaken together to make room for more, running over, and poured into your lap. The amount you give will determine the amount you get back.
Luke 6:38 (NLT)

Real Needs and Real Life

Prayers were always something that we needed. So many times I struggled watching my child face enormous difficulties, pain, and nausea. It was torture for me to witness. As a parent, I often wonder if I am doing everything I should be doing to rear my children correctly. I want them to be God-loving, happy, successful, and productive both now and as adults one day. I don't know if that is a question that a parent ever stops wondering. I only know that I haven't stopped thinking on it yet! I often wonder if I am setting enough of a Godly example every day, and I pray daily that I model the behaviors I want them to replicate. Am I maintaining and displaying Christ-like behaviors at home where they can see as much as I portray outside of the home and on social media? Am I demonstrating faith in my every-day conversations with them, keeping my cool under pressure, and taking advantage of every teachable moment to train them to live for Christ themselves?

I know I fail in some measure every single day, but I hope and pray that I am setting the very best example of living for God that I can so that if they behave as I do, it will be a good thing! Sometimes I get glimpses that we are being successful parents. These times are like beautifully-wrapped and beribboned presents floating down from Heaven in a stream of the brightest light and in the beak of a glimmering white dove. I feel this way when I notice one of the boys being especially giving to their brother, or when one of them quotes some Scriptural principal they have heard someone say. It is like a gift to me that encourages me to keep at it, and it make me feel so thankful.

One of the most traumatic parts of going through chemotherapy is losing hair. I think part of the reason it is so traumatic is because then it becomes obvious to everyone, even the people you don't know, that there is sickness. It can no longer be hidden, and you don't look like everyone else anymore. Men sometimes shave their heads when, due to age, their hair begins to let go in spots. This is certainly not the normal hairstyle for younger people, however, and at a time in life when trying to fit in is already difficult, hair loss becomes even more traumatic for pre-teens and teenagers.

While washing his hair in the shower at the hospital one afternoon, I heard Caleb cry out. I ran in to the bathroom and he shoved his wet hand beyond the white curtain and into my field of view. His palm and fingers were covered with hair. My eyes immediately filled with tears and my heart felt crushed. It was like a dose of reality settling in my heart, and it hurt worse because I could see how upset Caleb felt. His face mirrored mine. Looking back, I wish I had been able to find a more positive way to handle it than I did. I wish I had said, "That is so cool! You can have a shaved head like a tough biker dude! You are going to totally rock this!"

That was not what happened, however. I told him it was okay. I helped him wash his hair and watched it cake on my fingers and then flow down amid the stream of water and swirl around the drain as tears rolled down my cheeks. I left him to finish bathing and stepped out to inform Keith what was going on. I felt like I had been punched in the stomach by reality again. I had hoped this was not going to happen to him, though the medical professionals had all said that it was extremely probable that it would. Keith had even suggested shaving Caleb's head earlier and I had adamantly refused. I didn't want Caleb to appear like he was a sick child, one who was battling cancer, though I did permit cutting his hair really short.

Thankfulness for Keith

When Caleb got dressed and came into the room, I could see a spot about the size of a silver dollar on the top of his head where there was absolutely no hair. We had been warned that patients often were horrified when this fall-out began, and Caleb was no exception. He was very upset. I worked hard to keep my face composed, but Keith handled it like the champion he is. He explained to Caleb that it would be temporary, that his hair would grow back. He suggested it might even come back purple and all the kids in Alpha (the youth ministry at our church) would love it. Caleb just kinda glared at him. Keith pressed on and suggested that red would be kinda cool, too. Caleb responded that his dad was being goofy. He smiled.

Remember when I said that I often question if I am successfully rearing my boys? I got an indication that we were doing okay one afternoon shortly after Caleb began losing his hair. Caleb has a very independent personality – much like his mama. Joshua, however, needs a great deal more attention and physical touch in order to feel that he is loved. In order to help offer Joshua the support that he needs, Keith took him on a "daddy/son" date.

Keith took Joshua to lunch, Best Buy, and Game Stop, and then took him to get a haircut. Joshua sat down in the large swiveling chair and begin to talk to the stylist, explaining that he was spending time with his dad that day while his brother was getting chemo in the hospital. When she asked him what he wanted her to do with his hair, he asked her if she would shave him bald so that he could support his brother since he was going bald, too. Man! I don't know if I can even communicate the level of pride I felt in my youngest son when I received a text from Keith explaining what had happened with an attached photograph. Joshua is such an amazing boy, and he loves big.

We have pictures of both of them, arms around the other's shoulders, smiling, with not a strand of hair on their heads. At a time in life where appearance matters greatly, Joshua didn't want his brother to feel alone. This was how he demonstrated his love. And Joshua kept his head shaved, even in the coldest months. I crocheted a hat and scarf for both of them to help keep their heads and necks warm in the winter. They loved those hats. But more than the hats, I loved the affection that they showed one another. They knew things were so hard on everyone and each one went the extra mile to have a little more grace for the other. I was thankful.

Be Joyful. Be Thankful.

Scripture tells us in 1 Thessalonians, "Always be joyful. Never stop praying. Be thankful in all circumstances, for this is God's will for you who belong to Christ Jesus" (NLT). I do not always feel joyful, and I don't pray every minute of every day. I am thankful that there is a deep abiding joy that resides within me as a child of God even when my emotions are deceptively different. Father God is closer than a breath away any moment that I communicate with Him. But I am thankful that Scripture doesn't tell us to be thankful FOR all circumstances.

I am not thankful that my son was diagnosed with cancer. I am not thankful for cancer. Scripture does admonish that we are to be thankful and maintain an attitude of thankfulness IN every situation. That means there is always something for which I can be thankful, despite circumstances. Sometimes I have to look hard when I am in the middle of a storm. Sometimes, when circumstances are pelting me from seemingly every direction, my view is obstructed. But knowing how much God loves us enables us to wipe away the obstructions from our immediate field of view and see things with a clearer perspective.

There are always things for which we can be thankful, no matter the storms of life that swirl around us. Having that thankful attitude as part of our character helps us to maintain a positive outlook even if you feel rocked to the core. Friends and family help remind us that there is always something for which to be thankful as well. Jesus will be your solid ground. Oh, how firm a foundation!

7

Hope

This is my command – be strong and courageous!
Do not be afraid or discouraged.
For the Lord your God is with you wherever you go.
Joshua 1:9 (NLT)

I recently was driving down one of the many dirt roads where I live stopping occasionally to gather wild flowers to give as a gift to a friend. It was a beautiful, sunny April afternoon and the weather was perfect for the task at hand. There wasn't a cloud in sight in the bright, cerulean blue sky. I drove toward what used to be a beautiful pond, but the owner had drained it. Across the road from the pond was an old, run-down wooden grist mill and a spillway, the bottom of which was still full of water. I saw a turtle crossing in the middle of the road, and as he was so small, I felt quite intrigued by him. I stopped the car and got out to take a closer look and to take a picture.

As soon as I got out of the car, I watched him quickly slip into his petite, green shell. I walked up beside him, but didn't touch him because I didn't want to scare him further. I took some pictures with my hand beside him so that I could more accurately show his miniature size, and then waited for him to poke his head out of his shell. I waited for a couple of minutes and then figured he must still know that I am close by, so I backed up several feet so that I was just in front of my car. I waited several more minutes, but still he did not budge from his shell. I thought to myself that perhaps he could still see me somehow or sense that I was too close, so I got in my car and backed it up several more feet, turned off the ignition again, and waited for his head to protrude and for him to finish the short trek across the road.

I began to think of silly jokes that I could later tell my boys. "Why did the turtle cross the road?" I was standing there waiting on that turtle to cross the road while trying to come up with a response to the question a lot wittier than, "to get to the other side," but nothing was really coming to mind. I wondered if that turtle was ever going to move. I wasn't anywhere near him, and I had flowers to pick. I really needed him to hurry it up a bit.

My impatience won out. I returned to my car, turned the key in the ignition, and, giving the turtle a wide berth, drove around him and on down the orange clay road to finish gathering wild flowers for my friend. I figured once I was well out of his field of awareness, he would continue on his merry way, happily having avoided death once more. I also presumed that the likelihood of seeing him again was slim-to-none, and I was a bit disappointed that I wasn't able to watch him finish his walk across the road.

I continued panning the sides of the roads for vibrantly colored flowers. Seeing no more ahead after quite a distance, I turned the car around and headed back in the direction from which I had come so that I could look for more elsewhere. When I came back to the spot where I had seen the turtle, I was stunned to find him still sitting in the exact same spot he'd been in when I drove away many minutes earlier. I could hardly believe it.

I knew that I didn't have time to wait any longer, so I continued my flower-hunting expedition. I was determined to gather quite a few more flowers, but felt the Spirit of the Lord prick my heart about that turtle. The Lord told me that so many times, we, His children, get so bogged down in fear that like that turtle, we are unable to continue moving forward.

This turtle had his armor on, so he knew he was essentially safe if he stayed in his shell. But so captivated by fear, he was too paralyzed to make any progress toward his goal even when the potential danger had passed. The Lord asked me how many times I, too, had been like that turtle - too afraid to take the next step, get out of my comfort zone, or face a possible threat head-on.

Goals

In Philippians, Paul talks about how valuable a relationship with Christ is, stating that everything he'd ever done before knowing Christ as Lord was worthless in comparison to the pricelessness of serving God. He continues the chapter discussing how to walk out the Christian lifestyle, no matter the difficulties we face. He states:

> I have not yet reached my goal, and I am not perfect. But Christ has taken hold of me. So I keep on running and struggling to take hold of the prize. My friends, I don't feel I have already arrived. But I forget what is behind, and I struggle for what is ahead. I run toward the goal, so I can win the prize of being called to heaven. This is the prize God offers because of what Christ Jesus has done. All of us who are mature should think in this same way. And if any of you think differently, God will make it clear to you. But we must keep going in the direction that we are now headed. (Philippians 3:12-16, CEV)

Inwardly, I was cheering that turtle to keep going all the way until he had finished his journey and successfully crossed the road. But fear stopped him, and he had no other turtles nearby which, while pursuing their destinations, were going in the same direction and able to cheer him on. Nor was just their very presence able to set an example of safety and freedom by moving forward themselves.

I don't want to live like that turtle. He was covered with the protection he needed. I want to be moving forward toward the goals God has for me in my life. Ecclesiastes 7:8a reads, "Finishing is better than starting" (NLT). I want to finish what God has started in me, and I want to finish well.

Our Armor

Like that turtle, we, too, have spiritual armor that we should put on daily so that we have everything that we need to confidently face any battle that comes our way. Ephesians 6:11 tells us that we should "put on all of God's armor so that you will be able to stand firm against all strategies of the devil" (NLT). But the armor God provided us isn't so that we can hunker down and endure every attack of the enemy. Instead, He gave us an arsenal that allows us to move forward, protected, in the fight! Not one piece of armor covers our backsides, because we weren't made to retreat. Scripture does tell us, however, that there is power from attack on every side when we partner with another. Ecclesiastes 4:9-12 heralds the advantages of friends fighting by your side:

> Two people are better off than one, for they can help each other succeed. If one person falls, the other can reach out and help. But someone who falls alone is in real trouble. Likewise, two people lying close together can keep each other warm. But how can one be warm alone? A person standing alone can be attacked and defeated, but two can stand back-to-back and conquer. Three are even better, for a triple-braided cord is not easily broken." (NLT)

We were made to move forward into all that He calls us to do. Jesus did tell us that we would face trouble in the world, but He made every provision for us to overcome, just as He did himself. We were full of hope that we would win this battle. There were so many praying for us, standing beside us. And with an army of sword-wielding warriors by our sides, forward was where we were going.

Counts

When one is undergoing chemotherapy, "counts" becomes a very important word. Before any new round of chemo was begun, nurses would draw vials of blood and run some tests to make sure Caleb's ANC level was where it needed to be. ANC is the abbreviation for Absolute Neutrophil Count.

According to Dr. Kathleen Pagana, keynote speaker and author, neutrophils make up more than half of the total white blood cell count (2009). She states that infection and trauma elevate the white blood cell count. In an article I read by Dr. Pagana, I learned that a normal ANC "exceeds 2,500/mm3. A value above 1,000/mm3 usually means it's safe to continue chemotherapy. On the other hand, a value below 1,000/mm3 sharply increases the risk of infection. Neutropenia refers to an abnormally low ANC" (Pagana, 2009). The Children's Oncology Group (n.d.) breaks it down further, stating that if ANC counts are more than 1,000, there is a lower risk of infection; if the counts are between 500 and 1,000, there is a moderate risk of infection; and if the counts are lower than 500, that is the highest risk for the person to get an infection ("Low White Blood Cell Count (Neutropenia)," n.d.). So the higher his ANC was, the better. The lower the ANC, the more careful we had to be with him.

Depending on what his count was at the time of testing determined what procedures we were required to follow. He was placed on a neutropenic diet, which meant he couldn't eat fresh fruits and vegetables (unless they could be peeled - like a banana). He couldn't eat at buffets or salad bars. He was limited on what fast food he ate if any (no lettuce, etc.), and all of his foods had to be cooked very carefully with everything being very clean.

If his counts were low, he would have to wear a face mask when we were around crowds - like at the hospital or clinic. I remember Sundays when he had to wear a face mask at church, and he hated that. I was careful not to let him handle anything that could be harboring a lot of bacteria. I repeatedly told him, "Don't even think about touching those elevator buttons!" I carried hand sanitizer with me absolutely everywhere and he kept a bottle clipped to his belt loop as well. I reminded him to use it after nearly anything he handled. I had never before been so hyper-aware of germs. The diagnosis infiltrated every single aspect of our lives.

Revival

In the middle of November, the Bay of the Holy Spirit Revival was to be coming to our home church in Georgia. According to Wikipedia, The Bay Revival was rooted in the Brownsville Revival and was led by John Kilpatrick, pastor of the Church of His Presence, and Nathan Morris of "Shake the Nations" in Great Britain ("Bay Revival", 2016). A close friend of ours, Lydia Stanley (now Marrow), was leading worship for the Bay Revival. We were excited to see her and to attend the services, about which we had heard some pretty miraculous things!

The day came for the revival at church, and we started to get ready to go. Caleb's counts had been fine - no mask was needed; but just before it was time to go he started feeling very poorly. He said that he felt nauseated, tired, and his leg was bothering him. We found this to be very odd. He had not had any pain in his leg since the biopsy, and the tumor had already softened and even shrunk some from the original size of a cue ball to the size of a golf ball.

When it comes to church, attendance for our children was not an option they were given. It was and still is a very important part of their rearing. But if they didn't feel well, that was a totally different story. In those cases, one of us would always stay home with them. This time was different, however. The whole thing felt different. He had been fine until the first day of the revival and it felt like such an attack of the enemy - as though the enemy knew something good would happen if we went. After all, we had been saying for a couple of weeks on social media and to our family and friends that we felt a breakthrough was going to happen at this event. We were expecting something miraculous.

We bundled Caleb up and went to church. We sat toward the back and he laid down across several red cushioned chairs. The night was being broadcast on GOD TV and the time of worship was amazing. There was such a sense of peace, but there was also a sense that some mighty battles that we couldn't even see were being waged in the atmosphere. I kept my eye on my pale-faced Caleb and felt saddened that he was not feeling well. I wondered if I were doing the right thing bringing him to church. He would stand for a bit and then lie back down complaining that his leg was hurting where the tumor was located. He had also started limping pretty severely as we walked in that night – another new development.

Following the worship and a message, the evangelist began calling out specific health problems that people in the congregation might be facing, and then he would pray over those who came forward for prayer. We watched as God did some amazing things right in front of our eyes! One particular man had lost about 45% of the function of his lungs and was on oxygen. Following prayer, he was able to take big heaping breaths. He had not been able to do this before, and we had never seen anything like this in our lives.

The TV lights went out. The broadcast to the nations was over. But God was still moving. Evangelist Nathan Morris called for anyone else needing prayer. Caleb was hurting. He didn't understand why he was in so much pain, and Keith explained that he believed it was the enemy trying to keep him down, holding harder and not wanting to loosen his grip. The altar area was full of people but as the crowd began to thin down, I helped Caleb down the aisle to the area in front of the platform.

Nathan saw Caleb and summoned him onto the platform. Our pastor, Rich Bowen, was standing with him. He was praying. Nathan laid his hands on Caleb's stomach and began to speak out, "Cancer I curse you! You must leave this boy in the name of Jesus!" He then blew on Caleb, and Caleb's knees buckled and he fell to the floor.

From the back of the room, watching intently, Keith let out a yell of victory. He knew God was doing something amazing in our son. He made his way down the aisle with Joshua at his side and met us on the platform. Caleb was sitting up now and had a huge smile on his face.

He told us that when he fell down, such a peace washed over his body. He said that he felt a tingling fire in his leg where the tumor was, and that the pain was immediately gone. Nathan came back up to Caleb and kissed him on the forehead. He told us to let him know if we got any news from the doctors and prayed with all of us. Pastor Bowen hugged us and we returned to our seats.

Caleb reached down to feel his leg. He excitedly told us that he couldn't feel the tumor anymore! Keith and I both pressed against his leg, rubbing in the place where the bump had been. He was right! We could feel absolutely nothing!! The tumor was gone!

Healing

We were astonished by what the Lord had done. He had healed our son. We were seeing with our eyes the healing that Scripture declared. It was what we had spoken.

The following day, Keith called Caleb's oncologist and asked if she could schedule a scan. We were ready to see in black and white film the disappearance of the tumor - to see with our eyes that Caleb was healed! We were disappointed, however. The oncologist stated that no scan was scheduled but that even if she did one and it came back completely clean, Caleb would still be required to finish the chemotherapy regimen. They wanted to make sure that every cancer cell was gone, and there was no way to test for that.

Proverbs 15:22 reads, "Without counsel plans fail, but with many advisers they succeed" (ESV). Taking that word to heart, we sought the advice of our trusted friend and physician. He suggested we continue with the treatment as well, because the result of refusing treatment could be a lawsuit in which we could possibly lose the custody of our son. He encouraged us that we were not in the position of so many parents - wondering if the chemotherapy would work. We felt the cancer was already gone. Even though the treatment must continue, it wouldn't last forever, and the results were a done deal. It was not exactly what we had hoped to hear, but we certainly trusted our friend and the other physicians who had taken such great care of us thus far. But we knew the victory had already been won.

Testimony Time

The following night, we returned to the revival at church. Boy were things different! Caleb wasn't hurting at all that night! I could hardly believe the change that one touch from God had made. I'd never seen anything like that before, and had only read about those kinds of things in the Bible! And here we were, living the greatest miracle I'd ever known.

The evangelist asked Caleb to come to the stage that night to share what God had done. The testimony he gave was telecast all over the world on live TV and is still on YouTube today! He shared enthusiastically about what it had felt like when the Lord had touched him and how the tumor could no longer be felt. His dad and I confirmed the reports as well.

There was something so exceptionally fascinating to hear Caleb tell of what God had done so supernaturally. Part of it was the fact that this was my flesh and blood, my baby, standing there in front of over a thousand people in the sanctuary and who knows how many watching on TV sharing with such boldness and joy this thing that we could scarcely have believed if we had not been there ourselves to see and feel it. And part of it was that it was such a miracle! I had never known anything like it previously.

Pastor John Kilpatrick shared with our pastor that his young grandson had a prophetic word before the Bay Revival had even come to our church about an eleven-year-old boy with cancer in Augusta who was going to be completely healed. We didn't know that before Caleb was healed, and neither Pastor Kilpatrick nor Nathan Morris had ever met us and knew nothing about our story before the moment Nathan prayed for Caleb. That was just one more astounding aspect of the miracle.

We were so excited that we could not keep silent about this wondrous event. It felt like we were floating on cloud ten billion. The joy was unexplainable and absolutely bubbled over into everything we did that day as well.

Fever

Two days after he was healed, however, Caleb began complaining of a headache and sore throat. He had not yet seen the recording of his testimony, so he lay down on the brown sofa next to his dad to watch it. Keith put his hand on him and realized that he felt hot. He took his temperature. It was 101.3.

Earlier in this chapter, I explained about the ANC levels - the counts about which we had to be so careful. Chemotherapy kills the white blood cells along with the cancer cells, and it is the white blood cells that help our immune system to fight infections. The rule was if his temperature ever reached 100.5 degrees, we were to call the clinic and plan to come to the hospital. That is standard procedure. We called and reported his temperature, and were told to bring him to the ER immediately. We did, and spent the next four hours in a very small, very uncomfortable room away from the crowds.

One of my closest friends and her two boys came to the ER and brought us dinner. She stayed and visited with us, encouraging us with her words and her presence. Her boys helped to occupy our thoughts and our time as they talked with us. I still remember the little book bag her youngest had brought with him. It contained several items to help occupy his time along with items that are necessary for young people fighting diabetes. They had their own giants to face, but so sweetly made time to love on us. We waited together to see what would happen next, but clung with tenacity to Philippians 1:6, "Being confident of this very thing, that He who has begun a good work in you will complete it until the day of Jesus Christ" (NKJV).

Caleb's counts came back, and they were very low. They admitted him to the hospital. We felt that the low counts were a result of the chemo, and we hoped the doctors would tell us they would stop it.

Caleb's oncologist was not working during this hospital admittance. But we had always found the nurses and doctors caring for him to be capable and very smart. They were a little unsure about exactly what had caused the symptoms he was displaying, however.

At church the following Sunday, Keith was talking with our friend who is also a physician. Keith told him about Caleb's experience at the hospital after the miraculous healing. Our friend said that he had a theory about why Caleb's temperature had risen so drastically, why his numbers had crashed, and why his body was fighting so hard. He said that he would like to share it whenever Keith had time.

There's an old song with a line in it that says, "right now is the right time . . ." and Keith was ready to hear any wisdom our friend could share to enlighten us on the sudden turn of health. Keith was all ears as our physician and friend spoke. He asked Keith if he was familiar with "tumor fever." Keith said he wasn't, and our friend explained it to him.

Tumor fever is basically the name for when a large amount of tissue dies in the body - like when a tumor dies, suddenly, for example. The body absorbs that and then has to deal with ridding the body of the leftovers. The result would be fever, lowered ANC counts, and all of the symptoms Caleb had experience Friday night and Saturday morning. The hospital would have to treat the low counts quickly as an infection in a chemo patient could have very bad results.

Keith shared this information with me and we began to rejoice for even the fever! When Keith shared the theory with the attending physician, she agreed. She said that it made perfect sense as it explained all his symptoms. To us, this was more confirmation that the tumor had indeed died. The blood of Jesus had annihilated it!

Now it was time to focus on praying against the side effects of chemotherapy, as it was clear that the regiment was going to continue. We also felt very passionate about praying for other children who were fighting various health battles.

Now that we had seen God heal our son, we had no doubt whatsoever that He could heal anybody and everybody else.

At the end of his two-day stay, Caleb's counts were elevated to 6,500. We were excited about that because that is at the high end for a normal child. The oncologist decided to skip his next round of chemo so that he would be able to keep his counts up and even enjoy Thanksgiving!

Thanksgiving

That Thanksgiving was a very special one for our family. We had so much for which to be thankful, and we were full of hope about Caleb's future. Keith said that we had faced the biggest obstacle of our lives, in fact, he felt we had been hit broadside with it. God had given us a way for salvation and He had healed our son from one of the most dreaded diseases known to mankind. Many diseases you would have to call by name for people to know what you are talking about. But all you have to do is say, "the 'C' word" and people know to what you are referring.

Keith said that if God never did even one more thing for us ever, we would have enough for which to thank Him for the remainder of our lives. The fascinating thing, however, is that the Father's love for us, His children, isn't satisfied only in doing just "one" thing for us. If that were the case, all that Jesus endured leading up to the cross would have been unnecessary.

Salvation

The only thing required for salvation was Jesus's death. John 3:16-17 reads, "For God so loved the world that He gave His only begotten Son, that whoever believes in Him should not perish but have everlasting life. For God did not send His Son into the world to condemn the world, but that the world through Him might be saved" (NKJV). The cost for salvation was the life of His one and only son, Jesus.

Many learn why we should be saved and how to receive salvation by following the Roman Road. First, Romans 3:23 states "For everyone has sinned; we all fall short of God's glorious standard" (NLT). We all start on equal footing, we are all sinners - none better than another, and none of us are good enough to enter Heaven on our own merit. Romans 3:10 confirms that, "As the Scriptures say, 'No one is righteous - not even one'" (NLT). Romans 5:12 reads, "When Adam sinned, sin entered the world. Adam's sin brought death, so death spread to everyone, for everyone sinned" (NLT). So because we are all sinners, born into a sin nature and none righteous on our own account, death comes to us all. And our sin was a big deal as it separated us from God.

Hope is found in the next Scripture on the Roman Road, however. Romans 6:23 reads, "For the wages of sin is death, but the free gift of God is eternal life through Christ Jesus our Lord" (NLT). God designed for us a way of escape from endless death, and it is a free gift! Even though our sin separated us from God, because He loved us so much, He sent

His son to take our sin for us. Romans 5:8 explains this love further, "But God showed his great love for us by sending Christ to die for us while we were still sinners" (NLT). We, who are made in His image, are loved by God, the Creator of all!

So, we know that we are sinners separated from God, and that God made a way for us to be in right standing with Him when He sent Jesus to die for us, but what do we DO about it? Romans 10:9-13 reads, "If you confess with your mouth that Jesus is Lord and believe in your heart that God raised him from the dead, you will be saved. For it is by believing in your heart that you are made right with God, and it is by confessing with your mouth that you are saved. As the Scriptures tell us, 'Anyone who trusts in Him will never be disgraced.' Jew and Gentile are the same in this respect. They have the same Lord, who gives generously to all who call on Him. For everyone who calls on the name of the Lord will be saved" (NLT).

It is truly that simple! Asking Jesus, God's Son, to be Lord of your life and receiving the free gift of salvation is easy. To be saved, you simply pray aloud something like this: "God, I know that I have sinned and separated myself from you. I am sorry for my sins and ask you to forgive me for my sins. I believe that Your Son, Jesus Christ, died for my sins and that You brought Him back to life. I ask Jesus into my heart to be the Lord of my life from this day onward." If you believe your words in your heart, and have confessed Jesus with your mouth, you are saved! And with that gift received, there will be many others awaiting you as well. He is a such a good Father.

Asking Jesus, God's Son, to be Lord of your life and receiving the free gift of salvation is easy!
And with that gift will come many others.
He is such a good Father.

Gifts

But while salvation is the greatest gift we can ever receive, it isn't the only gift God wants to give to His children! God is a giver - it is His very nature to give good things. Matthew 7:11 speaks of His nature this way, "So if you sinful people know how to give good gifts to your children, how much more will your Heavenly Father give good gifts to those who ask Him" (NLT). I certainly want to give my children as many good things as I can! That being the case, God - who has perfect love for us - certainly wants to do even greater things for us than we could know!

One gift we had seen received by our son was the gift of healing. That was a gift that Jesus paid for before He even died. Isaiah 53:5 reads, "But He was pierced for our rebellion, crushed for our sins. He was beaten so we could be whole. He was whipped so we could be healed" (NLT). The King James Version states the same Scripture this way, "But He was wounded for our transgressions, He was bruised for our iniquities; the chastisement of our peace was upon Him; and with His stripes we are healed" (Isaiah 53:5). In the story of the crucifixion, we learn that Jesus was mocked, spit on, punched, had hair pulled from His face (reference Isaiah 50:6), was beaten with rods, and underwent a torturous Roman scourging. The beating and scourging produced the stripes on his back that purchased the healing for my son. I will not go into details of what a Roman scourging was like, but I cannot watch the graphic portrayal of it in The Passion of the Christ (2004 film) without thinking about how Jesus willingly endured all that torture so that my son could be healed. Scripture says He "gave Himself a ransom for all" (1 Timothy 2:6a, NKJV).

God had provided His Son, Jesus, so that we could be saved and have eternal life, but also so that we could obtain other gifts and promises as well. Our son was healed, and in time he was going to recover from all of the chemo. We knew God's purposes for Caleb would prevail, and could quote Psalm 118:17 confidently on behalf of our son, "I will not die; instead, I will live to tell what the Lord has done" (NLT).

Sharing the Good News

When you have something really wonderful happen to you, it is very hard to keep it to yourself. When people get a new puppy or a new car or house, they post pictures on social media so others can share in their excitement. When someone gets engaged or married, they can hardly wait to show off the new engagement ring or their new name! A new grandbaby born and there is no end to the pictures that get shared, even with complete strangers!

Merriam-Webster defines a miracle as "an extraordinary event manifesting divine intervention in human affairs" (n.d.). A miracle is so surprisingly wondrous, but because of its divine, supernatural nature it may be difficult for others to believe - especially if the person being told is skeptical about miracles occurring in our time. But when a miracle happens to YOU, it is hard to keep that level of joy internalized. It was positively something that we were excited to share with others as well.

I was looking for people with whom to share Caleb's story. In part due to my own excitement over his healing, but also to bring hope to others. I remember talking to an employee at a local pharmacy one afternoon. She wasn't in a rush and we just got to talking about life. Before long, the door opened for me to share with her what we had experienced with Caleb - that the tumor was there one minute and gone the next. There was no confusion or guessing what had happened to Caleb because we had experienced it first-hand, and sharing about what God had done with someone else rekindled the excitement afresh!

I remember patiently waiting with the boys in the sitting area of a car dealership one day as our vehicle was being repaired. Caleb's bald head and his coloring were such that an illness was fairly easy to identify by anyone. I could see a couple seated a few chairs down from us, and they kept looking in Caleb's direction with the most mournful expressions. Caleb noticed it too, and my shy boy spoke to them.

They acknowledged him and he began just to talk. Cancer came up, naturally, and as I sat back in my chair sipping on a cup of hot, scorched coffee with extra cream and sugar, my son started telling them all about how God had healed him! Their expressions changed from pitiful, to eye-popping, to enraptured. By the time Caleb had finished his story we all had tears in our eyes; amazed again at just how incredible God was Who had done this miraculous thing for my boy.

Testimony

Sharing our testimony helps people to overcome obstacles in their own lives because if God can do something amazing for *you*, then they begin to think that maybe God can do the same for *them*. And they would be right in thinking so. Your words telling of God's power in your life might be the very thing that buoys them through to breakthrough! Scripture also tells us in the book of Revelation that sharing our testimony defeats the devil and any influence he may try to exert in our lives.

The Message translation puts it this way, "They defeated him through the blood of the Lamb and the bold word of their witness" (Revelation 12:11). The "him" to which this verse is referring (and is referred to earlier in the passage) is the accuser of the brethren – the devil. It is because of the shed blood of Christ, so willingly poured out for us, that we have all that we need to have a victorious life. We also can be a depositor of that victory into the lives of others.

Your words telling of God's power in your life might be the very thing that buoys others through to breakthrough!

Because of all that God had done, I could see the boldness in us begin to grow. We didn't have to wait for Jesus Himself to come to earth and physically lay His hands on Caleb for the healing to be there. Jesus had already paid the price for Caleb's healing and because the Holy Spirit is present inside those who are saved, every child of God has been given the authority to do all that Jesus Himself did when He was on the earth! John 14:12 records Jesus saying, "I tell you the truth, anyone who believes in me will do the same works I have done, and even greater works, because I am going to be with the Father" (NLT). The new covenant, or promise, that Jesus established because of His death and resurrection gives brand new hope to us all and empowers us.

2 Corinthians 3:12 reads, "We have this hope, so we are very brave" (ICB). There is no priest or pastor we have to seek out to be our mediator when going to our Heavenly Father with requests. Ephesians 3:12 reads, "Because of Christ and our faith in Him, we can now come boldly and

confidently into God's presence" (NLT). And finally, like Paul in Acts 28:31, we can "proclaim the kingdom of God and teaching the things concerning the Lord Jesus Christ with full boldness and without hindrance" (HCSB). I love that God delights in our sharing about His goodness with others, and that He gives us the boldness to do so.

It's amazing that when you have good news to share it is easy to find an audience. Perhaps God ordains many moments for us to step into so that we are able to share what He is doing in our lives. When we are filled with the good things of God, it just pours out of us onto all with whom we come in contact. Sometimes it bubbles out in the form of a smile that shines brightly through our eyes clear to our joyful heart. Sometimes it comes in the form of laughter, or the urge to do random acts of kindness. It may even be tears of joy that sparks someone to inquire what we are feeling.

I know that even though there were still days of nausea, injections, hospital stays, cramped waiting rooms, tiny parking spaces in darkened garages, days of low counts, pain, and tears there was still an abiding joy in knowing that victory was already ours and we were full of hope toward a long future with both of our children. We couldn't keep that kind of news silent. It was made to be shared because there were other people to encourage.

It's amazing that when you have good news to share it is easy to find an audience.

We couldn't keep such joyful news silent.

8

The Proof is in the Pudding

The end of a matter is better than its beginning;
a patient spirit is better than a proud spirit.
Ecclesiastes 7:8 (HCSB)

God has also given us a desire to know the future.
God certainly does everything at just the right time. But
we can never completely understand what He is doing.
Ecclesiastes 3:11 (ICB)

The proof is in the pudding. According to the Grammarist website, this idiom means that "the end result is the mark of the success or failure of one's efforts or planning" (Proof is in the Pudding, 2014). In other words, you won't know if something was a good idea or not until you're finished and can view the end result (you don't know whether or not the pudding is good until you've tasted the pudding).

It is in our nature to want to know what the future holds. I've ridden down the road and seen many signs advertising fortune tellers. This, of course, being the enemy's counterfeit of true prophets of God who hear from the Spirit the good plans that God has in store for His people. He tries to mimic the things of God to bring confusion, distrust, or misbelief among people. But Scripture tells us that God Himself has placed within our hearts a desire to know our future (Ecclesiastes 3:11a). I hear this most commonly when people say, in the midst of a difficulty, "I just want to know that everything is going to be alright."

I've seen glimpses of some of the plans God has for me in my future – glimpses that are gifts of God to instill hope and a desire in me to keep pushing forward to attain all that He has for me. But He doesn't tell me everything that He is doing and every single step between my present and my future. This is where trust and faith in Him step in as I just walk out each step in my path as He guides me. Ecclesiastes 3:11b tells us, "God certainly does everything at just the right time. But we can never completely understand what He is doing" (ICB). He is always working on our behalf, and we will likely never know the intricacies of His moving for us on this side of Heaven.

While we were confident in what the Lord had done in Caleb, and had requested scans the day following the burning feeling in his leg, we had to wait for an additional three months before the next scans were scheduled. Waiting is not usually an easy thing when you are really looking for answers. We were anticipant for the scans, to say the least. The first procedure that day was an x-ray. The last time we'd had one of those, Caleb was in a lot of pain and I was anticipating a quick explanation and prescription before returning to church. Instead, we'd learned there was a much bigger mountain to face in front of us than we'd originally intended. It felt like we'd ridden a whole lifetime of roller coaster rides since then.

Proof

As soon as the x-ray was taken, we could see the results. The previous x-ray had clearly revealed a mass on his fibula (the smaller bone in the lower part of his leg). This time, however, as we stared at the x-ray, we saw nothing but bone. We were beside ourselves with excitement. When dealing with cancer, however, more in-depth scans are done so that physicians can see more than just the "big picture." They were looking not just for large masses but for smaller spots of cancer cells to see if any adjustments needed to be made in Caleb's treatment plan.

An MRI is a type of scan that gives different information than a bone scan, CT scan, or X-ray, and that was our next step. When the results came back from the MRI, the oncologists noted that they could see where the tumor was, but it was tiny and hard to distinguish. The bone scan that was completed showed that there were no other cancer cells visible anywhere else in his body, that the cancer had diminished, and had not spread. Our next step was for Caleb to undergo surgery so that whatever they saw in that scan could be removed.

Going Home

We moved back home before the surgery was to be done. We felt that we had gotten accustomed to the routines of treatment and were ready to return to an independent family unit again. This would give Keith's parents their own space back, as well. It felt so good to have our own personal space again, though I was thankful for all of the care we had received when we were living with Keith's parents.

The boys were glad to be home as well. Driving back and forth to work was much easier for me, but trips back and forth to the hospital and to clinic were going to be nearly four times longer for Caleb. He was coping fairly well with the treatments he was receiving, and we knew he would still able to rest at my in-laws' house if it was needed. We were thankful for all of the love and support that still surrounded us on every side from so many different people. Each one was a gift to us from the Father.

Keith and Caleb drove in to town to meet with the surgical team before the upcoming operation was to be done. I had returned to work and kept my phone with me every moment as I awaited news from the meeting. While my students were at lunch, I received a phone call from Keith.

Call for Surgery

He told me that the surgery would be the following morning and that the surgeon planned to remove a few inches of Caleb's fibula. The doctors stated that Caleb would be able to function just fine without the bone, so they would not install a rod or anything else in his leg to replace the part of the bone that they were removing. He was still growing and since metal rods don't grow, it wouldn't make sense to put one into his leg. That all sounded fine to me.

Then the hammer dropped.

Keith told me that the surgeon said he would have to sever the nerve that controlled the upward movement of Caleb's foot. That meant that he would no longer be able to lift his left foot, requiring him to wear a brace indefinitely. He said that there could be, however, a small plane of tissue around the nerve that he could cut away and would allow him not to cut the nerve, but that it would "take a miracle" not to have to sever it.

Caleb was immediately upset about this news and began to cry. Keith realized precisely where Caleb's mind was going as he was processing what the surgeon was saying. Caleb loves riding his four wheeler. If the nerve was severed in his foot, he would no longer be able to lift his foot to shift the gears. My brave boy was distraught, and I had not been there to comfort him.

Before leaving the meeting, Keith pressed the surgeon for more specifics – actual percentages - about the possibility of cutting the nerve on Caleb's foot. The surgeon told him that there was a 99.9% chance that the nerve controlling the upward movement of the foot would have to be severed and that it would take a miracle for him not to have to cut it. He also said that there were three blood vessels that run from the knee to the foot and that Caleb would lose at least one of them and possibly two. Losing two of them could possibly result in having to do an amputation. Having to sever all three would be a definite amputation. The vessels and nerves are all wrapped around the bone in that area, so it would be pretty much impossible that the surgery would end with nothing cut.

I processed all of this quickly-given information. How I perceived everything that I heard on a cell phone standing outside a noisy lunchroom full of energetic young school children talking with their friends still baffles me. I knew one thing - I would not be at work the following day. I would be at the hospital while my son was undergoing surgery. Keith knew something, too. We had a 0.1% chance of saving the motion in his foot. Not 1%, but 0.1%.

One percent would mean there was one out of 100 chances that the nerve would not be cut. That crazy odd is not even the degree of hope we were given. We are talking about point one percent. That is one tenth *of* a percent. One tenth of a percent means that there was one out of a thousand chances that the nerve would not be cut. That would be like this surgeon performing one thousand surgeries, and of those thousand, only ONE person would escape without that nerve being cut.

I don't even know what the likelihood was of the three blood vessels being cut, in terms of percentages. But all that Keith saw in that 0.1% was that there was hope. Caleb had a chance, and we knew exactly how to pray for our son. We were praying for 0.1%. We were praying for a miracle and we asked our family and friends to believe for this miracle with us.

Many times people look at the numbers, the possibility percentages, and think in negative terms. In Caleb's situation, it would be perfectly normal to think that the probability was stacked so highly against him. That the 99.9% was so close to 100% that the likelihood of cutting his nerves was conceded as fact instead of possibility. We even had a friend who was gracious enough to tell us that they could weld a handle onto Caleb's four wheeler for us so that he would be able to shift gears using his hands if he was unable to lift his foot anymore.

While the thought was coming from a place of generosity, I couldn't let my mind dwell on the possibility that the surgery would be anything other than a complete success. We couldn't give the chance of failure a place in our thoughts at all. Instead of looking at the percentage as if it were a problem, we looked at God and His ability to work a miracle on your behalf. No matter the percentages, He is more than able. Percentages don't scare God at all! Keeping our thoughts and our words focused on the most positive possibilities and in *His* ability kept our faith steadfast in the One Who had already proved Himself faithful.

Instead of looking at percentages as if they are a problem, look at God and His ability to work a miracle on your behalf.

Focus

In Scripture, we read that we don't fight battles the same way that world does, because we have access to "divine power to destroy strongholds" (2 Corinthians 10:4, ESV). Verse 5 of Second Corinthians 10 reads, "We demolish arguments and every pretension that sets itself up against the knowledge of God, and we take captive every thought to make it obedient to Christ" (NIV). Since Scripture, then, tells us that Caleb's healing had been provided already, we had to control what we allowed to be the focus of our thoughts. Clearly we had the power to accomplish this, otherwise Scripture wouldn't have told us to take our thoughts captive. So we continued to focus our thoughts and prayers on a successful surgery - one in which no nerves or blood vessels would be cut. One in which Caleb would keep his foot and the ability to move his foot. We focused on God's ability.

I am exceedingly thankful for the amazing physicians that I know and the ones who took care of Caleb, but this could not be a game of numbers. The numbers were not in our favor, but God certainly was. Romans 8:31 states, "What then, shall we say to these things? If God is for us, who can be against us?" (ESV). We were going to have to rely on the Great Physician to work a miracle on our behalf and trust Him to guide the physicians so that our son would come out of surgery with the use of his foot. Once again, we held on to hope.

The numbers may not be in your favor,
but God certainly is.

Surgery Day

The next morning, we arrived at the hospital bright and early. I'd love to say that I was completely confident, calm, and without any concern at all. While I was completely reliant on the Lord, I did have butterflies, but held my emotions in check so that Caleb didn't feel concern. Our pastor was there to pray over us before anything began, and our family was by our side as well. The wait began. The surgery took much longer than we had been told that it would, and I could feel tension building as the hours crawled by. Every once in a while, we would get a call from the OR to the nurse's desk to let us know that Caleb was doing fine and they were still working.

Several hours later, the surgeon emerged and called for Keith and me to join him in a separate room so that he could discuss the results of the procedure so far with us. We sat down on blue cushioned chairs, in perfect view of our parents on the other side of a wall full of windows. I was praying for good news as I could feel their intense gazes penetrating the glass across from us.

The surgeon told us that as he was cutting, he could see the nerves wrapped around the area in which he was working and was at dead-end. He said that he could see no way to avoid cutting through them, so before he severed anything he would stop, close his eyes, pray, adjust the overhead surgery lamp, and shift Caleb's opened leg. He looked rather shocked as he was telling us this. He continued explaining what had occurred in surgery, and his exact words were, "It was the craziest thing! I would adjust the light, and a new pathway around the nerves and blood vessels would emerge." He would adjust the LIGHT.

He said this happened several times in this exact sequence throughout the surgery. He paused, then said that he had not cut a single nerve nor any of the three blood vessels that he had felt so certain would be severed.

We had our miracle.

The surgeon also informed us that what they had seen on the bone in the MRI was just dead tissue from what was left of the tumor. He did say that we needed to continue to pray, however. He wasn't quite finished with the surgery, and he was cutting the bone and testing the marrow to make certain that it was normal. He said the readings were coming back abnormal, so he would keep cutting and re-testing to make sure that all traces of cancer were removed. He didn't want to cut too much bone away because it could still cause him to need to amputate Caleb's foot. Cutting the bone too close to the ankle could also weaken his ankle and keep him from being able to walk.

We had already seen the miraculous happen in this surgery and continued to pray for the surgeon and his team as he returned to the operating room where our son lay. A while later, the surgeon returned. He called us back to the same room and told us that he had continued cutting away at the bone and having it tested. He had cut away a total of about 10 inches of the fibula, and had stopped cutting about two inches above Caleb's ankle. The results of the tests were uncertain. If he cut further down the bone toward Caleb's ankle, he could severely limit the use of Caleb's foot. If it was still cancerous, he needed to go ahead and amputate the foot.

He told us that he went back and forth for about fifteen minutes trying to decide whether or not to go ahead and amputate that day in case it was cancer. But he took a moment and called the oncologist, who confirmed that what they were seeing could be one of two things. It could be the result of the sarcoma spreading, it could be the effects of the chemotherapy drugs, or the result of new marrow forming and not be cancerous at all. Both would look the same at first glance and they didn't have access to the technology on site that was needed to determine whether or not the samples were cancerous for certain.

The surgeon then called his mentor to discuss possible options and was told that if he could save as much leg as possible, they would be able to treat Caleb with radiation and get the samples thoroughly tested. He told us that he stopped and prayed about it, and felt impressed to do to Caleb what he would want someone to do if it had been his son on the table instead of ours. He did not amputate, but closed the wound instead.

Thankfulness

I could feel the tears of thankfulness pouring down my face. Keith had been holding on to me tightly as the surgeon had shared all that had happened behind the doors and beyond my reach. I could hardly believe that the surgeon had relied so heavily on prayer and had listened to what God thought about the matter at hand. I could hardly believe that the surgery was over and that we'd had so many miracles happen on Caleb's behalf. I could hardly wait to see my son in recovery. I could hardly wait to tell our youngest son, our parents, and our friends all that God had done for us all. Our prayers had been answered. None of the nerves or vessels had been cut and Caleb still had his foot. The goodness of God was so tangible in that moment. So good that it was almost unbelievable.

I wonder how many times in life, we get so bogged down in possibilities and probabilities in the situations that we sometimes find ourselves. How many times do we not even consider the fact that God is more than able to do something miraculous for us as a result of looking at the natural facts. Sometimes, like the surgeon did however, we need to stop and pray. And then perhaps let the truth of God's Word shine a light on our situation. Perhaps in doing so, a new path will become clear to us, as well.

Years later, Keith ran into that surgeon at a local store. As Keith and the surgeon were talking, he told Keith that he was still in awe over what all had happened with Caleb's surgery. He said that he loved to tell others about what a miracle he witnessed that day. He knew that the all-powerful God had been working through him!

Recovery

We didn't have to wait too terribly long to see Caleb. While our parents continued to entertain Joshua, Keith and I were escorted to the recovery area. Caleb was in a very chilly room being administered morphine by a very friendly nurse who was hard at work getting Caleb as pain free as possible. Caleb was hurting quite a bit after the lengthy surgery, and it took many morphine doses to get him comfortable. The first thing we did was to tell Caleb to lift his foot – an action we had been assured would be impossible after the surgery. Caleb stared down at his foot and watched almost in disbelief as he pulled his toes toward him and away. He was watching the impossible happen with his own eyes.

After Caleb was stable, he was taken to the PICU, where the surgeon came to check in on him. He was very surprised to see that Caleb was awake and responsive to him.

He moved the blanket away from Caleb's left leg to check for any feeling. He said he didn't expect Caleb to be able to move his foot at all because even though the nerve hadn't been cut, the surgeon and his team had probably bruised it and several lesser nerves as he moved them around. He said that it would likely take some time for Caleb to be able to respond to stimuli. He reached down and used his pen to touch the bottom of Caleb's foot, and Caleb responded by pulling his foot back at the ankle. The surgeon was completely surprised! Caleb was even able to wiggle his toes and his foot. This was supposed to be impossible so soon after surgery, but with God, nothing is impossible.

God is in Control

God gave us many signs over the next few days that He had us in His complete care. When Caleb had first been diagnosed, one of the nurses who took such great care of all of us was Veronica. She had been amazing, and had even prayed with us in his hospital room after we had first received the diagnosis. Well, when we looked up to see the nurse who would take care of Caleb in the PICU, it was Veronica who walked through the door! We were so excited to see her, and felt the Lord had blessed us with her because He knew she would be exactly what we needed in the week spent in the hospital recovering from surgery.

The next morning, Keith sent me downstairs to grab breakfast and get a change of scenery for a few minutes. My meal cost $7.77 after tax. I've always heard that the number seven represents a holy number and that God repeats things if it is something that would likely come to pass quickly. (Think in terms of the multiple dreams had by Pharaoh that indicated a famine would be coming to the land and how God used Joseph to interpret those dreams and how they came to pass just as he said they would. It is in that passage of Scripture that we learn that dreams repeated mean they will happen soon.)

I was indeed paying attention when the total for my meal was such an unusual amount, a number repeated thrice. I have a book written by Ira Milligan that was recommended to me by one of my best friends. The book is entitled, The Ultimate Guide to Understanding the Dreams You Dream, and I use it along with prayer to help determine if there is something specific the Lord might be trying to reveal to me when I dream. When I recently looked up the number seven in this dictionary of dream symbols with Scriptural references, it states, "Complete: All; finished; rest" (Milligan, 2012). It was like the Lord was reminding me that He was in perfect control of the situation with Caleb and the we could rest knowing He would complete the work He had begun. Since this is a Scriptural principal (Philippians 1:6), I knew that I could trust it.

A Setback

Caleb was recovering well, and we were still amazed at the many miracles God had performed. Five days after surgery, we were discharged and went to the pharmacy on our way home to get the pain medications Caleb would require. I went inside the drugstore holding the prescription papers and awaited them being filled. As I was waiting, I was browsing several aisles. I heard a noise and, looking up, saw Keith running toward me. Alarmed at his unexpected appearance, I ran to him as he began to tell me that we had to go.

Caleb had gotten sick in the car and was grabbing his head and crying loudly. Crying is so uncharacteristic of Caleb that we knew this was serious, and we rushed back to the hospital. The whole way there, he was gripping his head and crying out in pain. I was a nervous wreck, frantic because there was nothing I could do to help my boy.

I wished I could have simply snapped my fingers and caused the pain to dissipate or make us instantaneously arrive at the emergency room. I am thankful that we were not far away. He was seen in the ER as soon as we arrived. The emergency room staff administered the very pain medication we had been waiting on at the pharmacy. They also did some blood tests and completed a CT scan.

While we waited for the results of the tests, Keith posted what was happening on social media and requested our family and friends to be praying. A friend suggested that she had experienced several similar symptoms after receiving an epidural when she was having a baby. She said that she almost didn't say anything to us about it, but felt prompted by the Lord to do so. Keith thought about it and recalled that when Caleb was being prepped for surgery, the anesthesiologist had told us that he had attempted an epidural on Caleb twice and had missed so they had used an alternative form of anesthesia for the surgery.

All the tests results from the emergency room were coming back clear. Keith mentioned the failed epidurals to the ER physician and mentioned what our friend had told him about experiencing similar symptoms when she'd had an epidural before giving birth. The physician began nodding his head and stated that would be consistent with the symptoms Caleb was experiencing. Turns out that it was an issue of spinal fluid leaking that was causing the intense pain. The doctor said that they could repair it surgically, or we could go home and allow him to rest and it would repair on its own. We chose the latter route, and after a couple of days Caleb was headache free.

Post-Surgery

Caleb was learning to use his crutches, though we had to fuss at him to use them so that his leg could heal properly. The hospital staff had sent someone to our room before we were released to teach him (and us) how to properly use them to get around. Keeping a young boy immobile is quite a feat, and as young children generally consider themselves invincible – making him use the crutches was equally difficult. We were still waiting on the results to come back from the abnormal marrow they had removed in surgery so we would know if he would have to have radiation. It seemed there was always something to pray about and even more for which to be grateful.

Thirteen days after surgery, we had a follow-up with Caleb's oncologist. She said that she was very excited about how well Caleb had responded to the surgery. She said that she was even more excited with the preliminary results of the biopsy of the "abnormal" bone marrow that had been tested. She said that they would need to double check their findings before issuing an "official" report, but that it looked like all they were seeing as "abnormal" was actually just dead tumor cells and where the healthy bone marrow had been regenerating. God had indeed incinerated the tumor and caused new marrow to grow. Based on their results, Caleb would NOT be receiving any radiation! We had the proof!

The Proof is in the Pudding

We were thrilled with this news. We had another twenty-two weeks of chemotherapy ahead, and were praying that there would be no complications that would make it take any longer than absolutely necessary. We received confirmation of the work God had done on March 8th. The tumor they had seen on the MRI and had removed was 100% dead. God never does anything halfway. He had done a mighty and complete miracle. And what He did for us, He can do for you.

Our God is mighty.
He never does anything halfway.

Healing Time

Caleb's incision had some minor infection and the skin that should be sealing and scabbing over was separating. We treated the wound very carefully by packing it with sterile gauze soaked in saline solution. It was not fun to say the least, but we were so encouraged by all that God had already accomplished that it was impossible to feel downhearted for long.

Caleb's endurance was mind blowing to me. Packing the wound and keeping it sterile was tedious for me but excruciatingly painful for him. I'm sure you have heard the expression, "It's like putting salt on the wound" referring to someone hurting you in an area in which you've already been hurt. Well, that is precisely what I was doing to Caleb. I was putting saline (salt) solution in an open wound. The process that would heal the severely opened wound was causing him inordinate amounts of pain.

I could hardly believe all of the obstacles he had faced and overcome already. The illnesses, surgeries, medicines, hospital stays, clinic visits, injections - I could scarcely imagine getting through all of that as an adult - even a portion of what he had already gone through. But he faced it with a positive attitude like a champ. We focused on conquering the twenty-two weeks that were ahead of us and looked for ways to have fun in the meantime. We still had work ahead, but the promise had already been acquired, and we had the proof.

We've Got the Proof. Where's the Pudding?

Caleb was scheduled to participate in our local Relay for Life later that spring. We had participated in this event as supporters in previous years, but this year it would hold more personal meaning. He would be honored as a survivor. The week of the Relay for Life came. The school in which I taught works all year fundraising for cancer research, and this year the need for a cure had hit closer to home. My co-workers had been so encouraging, and I received several texts throughout the months of treatment with pictures of fundraising activities that were done specifically with Caleb in mind.

Caleb was scheduled to be receiving chemotherapy in the hospital the week of Relay for Life. That would mean he would be limited in his ability to participate in the events, if he was able to participate at all. We had also received four tickets to a NASCAR race in Talladega as a gift. Keith hoped to take both boys and a friend (because people generally frown upon my disinterested crocheting during a race - they just don't get it). But if Caleb underwent chemo the week before, his counts would be too low to participate in such crowded events as he would be susceptible to infection. It wasn't a risk we could take.

Keith called and talked to one of our lead oncology nurses to see if we could adjust his schedule. He explained how important it was to Caleb to be able to participate in Relay for Life and to be able to go on this guy - trip to cheer on his favorite driver. She assured us that she would do everything that she could to make this happen for Caleb.

Keith took Caleb in to the clinic and they drew blood to check his counts. They wanted to see if they would need to supplement his numbers by giving him blood or anything else to boost his numbers. The counts came back from the lab, and they were all high enough for him to not only receive an all-clear for participating in the weekend's activities, but he also didn't need anything to supplement his counts! Caleb was so excited!

The night of the Relay for Life came, and I remember feeling so emotional. We all had tears in our eyes as we prayed together and then watched Caleb walk that lap around the track. That he could walk at all, lifting both of his feet, walking and bearing weight on both of his limbs – it was amazing. He was literally a walking miracle. We joined him on the walk, noting the luminaries which had been purchased and lit in his honor.

After we finished participating in the Relay for Life activities, the boys loaded up and headed to Talladega. They were so excited! I cannot understand the depth behind all of their excitement. NASCAR just isn't my cup of tea, but it was clearly spilling out of their eyes! Keith hoped to be able to acquire pit passes so that they would be able to get close to the cars and drivers before the race.

The Race

When the boys arrived at the campground near the track early the next morning, they set up the camper and went right to sleep. When they awoke, they were busting to get their day started, as the track was full of fun activities for all ages. Caleb and Joshua were given some money from their Uncle Wayne to purchase new racing hats, and as they each have a different "favorite driver" they enjoyed the quipping back and forth that men seem to find so thrilling. Keith was able to get pit passes, and they went to bed after the first night of racing anticipating getting up close to some of their favorite drivers.

The next day was stormy looking, but the thunder rumbling in the background and the rain falling on the way to their seats didn't dampen their spirits in the slightest. Keith had sent a message on Twitter to someone who was a close contact of Caleb's favorite driver, Jimmie Johnson, in the hopes that they would be able to see him. He was told that they'd see what they could do about Caleb getting to see the Lowe's racing driver up close, but they couldn't make any promises.

Caleb's leg started bothering him from all the walking the day before, and guest services provided a golf cart and staff driver for them to use to get out of the pits and back up toward their seats since the pits were about to close. On the way, Keith received a text that Jimmie Johnson was scheduled to be at the TV truck in the pits around 11:00, and that Keith should come. Again, there was no promise that they would absolutely see Jimmie Johnson, but there was a chance.

The guest services driver turned around and took them right back, and though they didn't have credentials to get them into the deeper parts of the pits past closing time, they managed to get by since they were being driven by track personnel! They were dropped near the meeting area and waited. After a few moments, Keith's friend punched him in the arm and announced, "There he is!!!" Keith turned around and sure enough, there was the man himself getting off a golf cart with his hand extended toward him.

Jimmie Johnson took time out of his busy schedule before the race to spend some time talking to them and taking photos with the boys. Caleb was astounded. It was a moment they wouldn't likely forget in their lives. The weekend was more than anyone could have imagined and exactly the break he needed before chemotherapy began again.

I have heard many times that God will not put more on you than you can bear, that He will make a way of escape for you. That common phrase is taken from Scripture found in 1 Corinthians. The Message translation puts that verse this way, "No test or temptation that comes your way is beyond the course of what others have had to face. All you need to remember is that God will never let you down; He'll never let you be pushed past your limit; He'll always be there to help you come through it" (1 Corinthians 10:13, MSG).

God is so faithful. And He is into the details of our lives. I love that He worked out all of the details of their weekend. He had seen Caleb and our family through so many difficulties, and was always at our side.

He never let us down. He was there to shoulder the burdens so that we didn't have to carry them. He had performed so many miracles, as we spoke out in prayer, praise, and in declarations the various Scriptures on which we were standing. With every miracle that we saw, we understood that it was a result of God's goodness and love for us. It was the truth of His Word coming to life. We weren't any more special to Him than anyone else. He loves you every bit as much as He loves us. Oh the wonders He wants to perform on our behalf! It was a sweet thing, and we had the proof.

God shoulders our burdens
so that we don't have to carry them.
Miracles are a result of God's goodness and love for us.
It is the truth of His Word coming to life.

9

Dream Big

God can do anything; you know –
far more than you could ever imagine or guess
or request in your wildest dreams! He does it not by
pushing us around but by working within us,
His Spirit deeply and gently within us.
Ephesians 3:20-21 (MSG)

Even in the hospital, there were moments that were like little gifts fluttering down from our Heavenly Father. Caleb enjoyed playing electric guitar, and sometimes even brought it to the hospital with him to help him occupy his time when he was getting treatment. On one stay, the children's hospital had a professional musician, Mr. Joe, come to play for the children.

Caleb was talking with the Mr. Joe and told him that he liked to play guitar, too. Mr. Joe handed him a guitar and asked what songs Caleb knew. Caleb started playing "Sweet Home Alabama." Mr. Joe told him that his band was going to play that very song for all the children later in the program in the hospital lobby. All of the children were given a variety of instruments - bongos, maracas, and hand drums to play along with Mr. Joe, but Caleb was given a guitar.

After the program, Caleb and Mr. Joe were talking. Caleb was telling him that he had left his guitar at home but that his mom was going to bring it to the hospital later in the week. He told Caleb that no guitarist should ever be without a guitar, so when Caleb returned to his hospital room, he had one of Mr. Joe's guitars in his possession with the charge to take good care of it until Mr. Joe returned to pick it up. Caleb spent days playing that guitar in his hospital bed and never mentioned being bored for a moment!

A month later, Caleb got to sit in with the worship band during rehearsal at church. He was so excited, nervous, and overwhelmed! He later said that he didn't know a lot of the chords, but Keith assured him that was why he was at rehearsal - to learn. It was absolutely thrilling to me and to Keith to have both of our boys attending the rehearsal. Joshua was practicing singing with the guys on the praise team with me, and Caleb was playing in the band with his dad. It was one of those precious moments that we were able to see the desire to fulfill their calling to serve the Lord. Doing so as a family made it even more precious.

Brighter Days Ahead

There were many ups and downs over the next few weeks. We dealt with oozing mouth sores, good counts, low counts, EKGs, blood transfusions, hospital stays, injections, chemo, nausea, and exhaustion. We were so tired of all of the trips to the hospital and clinic, tired of the treatments, tired of it all. But it was good to see the number of weeks remaining in treatment getting smaller and smaller, and we were dreaming of brighter days ahead.

We hit the nine-week mark. There were nine weeks remaining of chemotherapy. We could see light at the end of the tunnel. I was on my summer break from school. What I wanted to be doing was going on family trips, though Caleb had no desire to return to the warm, sunny, breezy beach. Summer is the most ideal time for teachers to plan on yearly check-ups and dental visits of their own as they don't need to ask for time off. I did this as well, working in a yearly checkup for myself around Caleb's chemotherapy.

Doctor Visit

I truly dislike going to the doctor. I don't typically go unless I feel there is no way to avoid it, but I was trying to be very careful about my own health since I was having to be so careful about Caleb's. I was talking with my physician as she was looking me over.

Yes, I knew I needed to eat less ice cream and try to exercise more. Yes, I knew that the weight listed on my driver's license didn't match the scale in her office. UGH. I hate going to the doctor. I especially don't like getting my finger pricked and they insist on that torture every single time that I go. I contemplated "pulling a Caleb" and throwing a fit.

There was nobody there from my family to hold me down. I smiled as I thought about how far he had come, and sucked it up while I stuck out my hand.

The doctor paused as she noticed a spot on my abdomen. She said that given my son's history, she would like to remove and biopsy the spot. Part of me started to panic. We were still dealing with chemotherapy for Caleb. There was no way I could do this right now. I had to be there for him! I couldn't be taking treatment at the same time as my twelve-year-old! My mind reeled far down the wrong road.

It was then that I realized that I was believing the worst possibility and succumbing to fear instead of standing in faith. The moment you feel your mind imagining the worst possible scenario is the very moment you can trust that thought doesn't come from God. God is not the author of fear, and we all are able to control the thoughts we dwell on.

The moment you feel your mind imagining the worst possible scenario is the very moment that you can trust that thought doesn't come from God.

The reason that I know this is fact is because God wouldn't ask us to do something that was impossible for us to do! 2 Corinthians 10:5 commands, "Casting down imaginations and every high thing that exalts itself against the knowledge of God, bringing every thought into captivity to the obedience of Christ" (MEV). I knew better than to let my imagination wander like that.

At that moment, I realized that I was dwelling on fearful, ungodly thoughts, and just as quickly I understood from where those thoughts were coming. Realizing that, I felt such a peace wash over my whole body. I focused, instead on the realization that the God Who had done so many miracles already for my family was right there with me. I felt the Lord tell me in that instant that I was okay, and I knew like I knew my name that there was no cancer in my body. I asked my doctor if the biopsy was something that needed to be done that day, and she said that it could wait a day or so. She said they would schedule it to be done in her office later that week.

I went home and told Keith what had happened. While it is in my nature to sweep things under the rug and not face a potential problem, we knew the possible seriousness that caused the doctor concern and knew that we needed to face it. While I felt positive that it was an unnecessary procedure, I called and made an appointment just the same. In my mind, the purpose was just to prove that what I felt the Lord saying to me about my body was true and to eliminate with finality any concern over my health.

A friend from work said she would go with me since the biopsy was scheduled on a day that Caleb was receiving treatment. There was no finger prick for me that day, and I was pleased as punch about that. I was armed with Godly confidence and Caleb's tube of anesthetic cream to numb the area on my abdomen so that I wouldn't feel the injections with which she planned to administer the numbing medication before the biopsy procedure began.

I laid flat on the table at her office looking at the cut-out of the doctor's family from a magazine that she had framed on the wall over me. I only felt a few pinches, thankfully, and didn't think about the incisions she was making as she removed the spot that was to be tested. The time we spent waiting on the wound to heal and for the results of the biopsy seemed, in some ways, familiar. But I had an amazing sense of peace as I felt the Holy Spirit whispering to me repeatedly, "I will not put more on you than you can bear. Do not worry. Do not be afraid. You are just fine." So I chose to obey that voice and rested in the knowledge that God was my healer and my foundation. A few days later, we received confirmation that I was all clear. There was nothing to the spot at all.

Camp Rainbow

We kept our focus on all the good things that were going on around us - every blessing, and there were many. The boys would be attending Camp Rainbow for a whole week, and they were very excited. Camp Rainbow is a week reserved for children facing cancer, included siblings, and is intended to give them as much hope, encouragement, fun, games, and candy as they can contain! The boys wouldn't be in the same cabin, but instead would room with children in their own age group. They would ride bicycles on trails, climb obstacle courses, take canoes and paddle boats out on the lake, shoot bows and arrows, make crafts, shoot rockets in the air, have musical guests perform for them, ride horses, swim in a massive pool, and even participate in a dance at the end of the week.

I was concerned about being away from them both for so long as neither of them had attended any kind of overnight camp previously. It was even more disconcerting because we had to be so careful with Caleb. He had a variety of medications and routines that had to be followed to the letter, and his dad and I were not invited to camp.

The head nurse and the director of the camp both talked with me regarding the experience and assured me that the boys would be extremely well cared for. There would be oncology nurses, doctors, and hospital staff available every moment the whole week, and they were the same medical professionals who were already familiar with Caleb and his particular situation. They were even equipped to administer chemotherapy on site if it was scheduled. Knowing that all the nurses and some of the doctors who were so intimately familiar with Caleb's journey were going to be at the camp helped tremendously in my allowing him to attend. We also had the opportunity to form many friendships among the family members of other children fighting cancer at the clinic and hospital, and most of those children were also going to camp.

We spent a week packing and labeling everything the boys could possibly need for a week of camp. There were towels, washcloths, clothes, sandals, sneakers, bug spray, sunscreen, hats and sunglasses, flashlights, and other knick-knacks. Joshua made certain to pack a red t-shirt for every single day of the week - not because he particularly favors red, but because the director of the camp despised it. Mrs. Kym had made that point many times over, including mentioning the fact that her hair was NOT red. (Perhaps we should just refer to it as a warm auburn to be safe.) She wouldn't even say the word red, but would spell it out. She is one of the funniest people I've ever met and if her job was solely keeping the children laughing, she did it quite successfully. My boys adore her.

The day came when we hauled tremendously large and heavy duffle bags, pillows, rolled sleeping-bags, and a bag full of medication to the children's hospital. There were two large busses on the street beside the hospital, and a crowd of families checking in and excitedly talking about the activities the coming week would hold for the children. No one seemed worried in the slightest, but I felt pinches of concern at the coming separation.

I smiled for pictures with the boys, but the tears pricked the corners of my eyes. Several of our friends and fellow chemo-families patted my back and reassured me that the boys were going to have the time of their lives and wouldn't be missing me at all. I could see my boys through the tinted windows of the bus and they were signing with their hands and mouthing out the words that they loved me. I smiled big at them like I was so excited that they were able to go, but a few tears slipped down anyway. I hastily brushed them aside, and grinned even bigger for their sakes - returning words of affection to them.

Keith was at my side as the busses pulled away, and we stood there waving even as other parents began wandering slowly back to their vehicles. I had worked two extra weeks at the beginning of the summer, and had put that money aside so that Keith and I could have a short trip the week the boys were at camp. We got into our car, and I spent the first several miles of our trip crying.

Keith took the same route out of town that the busses had gone, and we caught up to them as they turned off the interstate onto the exit that would take them to camp. I was thankful for my husband's thoughtfulness to get me one last glimpse of the children, then I dried my eyes and focused on our destination. I could hardly wait to dig my toes into the warm beach sand once again. It felt like ages since I'd been able to do that.

Coming Apart, Not Falling Apart

We spent four days at the beach relaxing and not administering medication or thinking about carefully cooking meals or checking on the children or how any little decision we made could affect Caleb. It was a much-needed time of refreshing and just being a couple. It had been such a long time since we'd only had each other to consider. I remember our pastor stating that sometimes we needed to come apart before we come apart! The days of separating ourselves from the strenuous routines and just resting and enjoying the company of the other was most restorative.

I am so glad we were able to make the trip, but I was also looking forward to seeing my boys and hearing about their experiences. When they returned to the hospital for pick up, we were there waiting for them. We were a little sun kissed and smiling from ear to ear. So were they!

They talked non-stop about all of the activities in which they had been able to participate during the week, and I was so thankful that we had all had time to get away from the painful procedures that had become so customary for a while. Caleb had even had an opportunity to be on the local news. Keith had been told to make sure that Caleb brought his guitar to camp and had been let in on a little secret that Caleb would discover at camp. Keith encouraged Caleb to work out the guitar parts on a song called "Shine" by the group Collective Soul - an Atlanta-based rock band. When he went to camp, Caleb was asked to play with his musician friend Mr. Joe and his band in front of all his peers. (Mr. Joe was the man who had loaned Caleb his guitar at the hospital several weeks prior.)

Later that evening, Caleb played on stage with the lead singer from Collective Soul! He played the main guitar part on the intro and throughout the song. He said that he was very nervous and had a hot stage light on his face. It made him feel like a bona fide rock star! We were delighted to receive a video of the week's activities, including excerpts from the concerts in which Caleb had participated. It was such a good week for everyone and we were so thankful that the boys were able to attend. We had no idea how healthful and recuperative the week would be for each of us.

Have a Dream? Work Hard!

Caleb was persistent in practicing guitar. I never had to ask him to practice; it was just a strong, innate desire. One weekend, Keith was asked to lead worship at a local church while their worship pastor was out of town. The bass player was also going to be out that Sunday, so Keith asked Caleb if he wanted to learn to play bass and fill in.

Caleb jumped at the opportunity to play with his dad, and I remember walking behind them snapping photos as we entered the church that morning - Keith with his stool in one hand and Caleb with a borrowed bass in his. The church gave Caleb a small financial gift for his service and Caleb was so excited to get a check made out to him! It was his first paying gig, and it wasn't something he'd even considered might happen! Keith and I were so proud that Caleb was able to share the platform with his dad - playing and doing such a great job helping with worship. He enjoyed it so well that He decided to spend more time practicing bass, and it wasn't long before he found that he had real skill with it.

That gig turned out to be such an unexpected blessing. Musically speaking, Caleb was learning electric guitar and playing on the piano some. But he had never considered changing his instrumental focus. That was the beginning of an unexpected revelation of a new passion and dream for him.

If I thought he spent a lot of time practicing electric guitar before, that was nothing in comparison to the passion he had for bass. He had such a feel for the rhythm and notes, and listened to many inspiring and talented bassists. He would listen to exactly what they played and then emulate what he heard. He would play along with the music over and over, repeating sections until it reached perfection. With his musical gifting (absolute pitch) and persistence in practicing, his skills multiplied almost exponentially.

A New School Year

Summer gave way to fall - my favorite season of the year. It always reminds me of one of my favorite movies in which one of the actors talks about how the fall makes him want to purchase school supplies. In the movie, he says in an email to the leading actress that he would "send you a bouquet of newly sharpened pencils if I knew your name and address" (Ephron,1998).

That sounds pretty ideal to me. I love sharpening brand new, colorful pencils and having them ready to distribute to my students on the first day of school. I love the smell of new books, the joy of setting up my classroom, rehanging the curtains, and getting everything ready. I love seeing the names of the students who will be mine and arranging name-topped desks in preparation for them. I love setting up my gradebook and filling in the squares in my lesson plan book for the very first time after so many months. And it was that time of year again.

We had discussed what to do with the boys for the following school term as I was preparing to return to the classroom myself. Since Caleb was not yet finished with chemotherapy, continuing to homeschool them would be the best thing. We enrolled them into an online public school so that the majority of their schooling wouldn't be as time consuming for us as I was working and Keith was spending most of his time as caregiver for Caleb. He was picking up odd jobs to help supplement our income, as well, and he found teaching rather taxing. Using an online option would help him to focus on more important things.

The boys would both need access to computers and considering the amount of time that they had to spend away from home, laptops were needed for both of them. The Lord was already aware of the fact that we had one and needed another, and He had a plan to take care of that. Without our even asking anyone for anything, the social worker for the children in the Pediatric Oncology/Hematology department contacted a computer company and they sent a brand-new laptop to us to use on a two-year lease at no charge!

God is always aware of our every need and His timing is impeccable, and we were in awe yet again of His love for us. He is into the details of our lives, and this was just another example of God's faithfulness. So, the boys were completely set up and ready to go - they could enjoy the last few days of their summer break. Caleb had only a few more weeks of chemotherapy to receive and we could hardly contain the excitement.

God is always aware of our every need and His timing is impeccable!

Focusing on the Important Things

In the routine of trips back and forth to the hospital and clinic for treatment, it is easy to lose count of what treatment number you are receiving. The countdown was definitely on, however, as we anticipated the cessation of chemotherapy and a return to a more normal life. We have found that when God does miraculous things for you, it is hard to return to life as "normal." We began to see so many things much differently now than we did before.

I have a deeper appreciation for my family and friends who stood in the fire with us. I have a more passionate awareness of what really matters in life. As a teacher, I was always all about the boys excelling in school, writing complete sentences in their best handwriting, scoring well on assignments, and being thorough in their studies. While schooling is important, I'd discovered that there is so much more to life than school. It just doesn't consume my thoughts like it did before, and I began to spend a lot more time looking for God's hand in our everyday lives.

I think tragedy in any form often refocuses on the things in life that really matter. When someone you love receives a bad diagnosis, a job is lost, a loved one who has passed on from this life to the next, when flood waters rise and it seems you have lost everything you've worked so hard to attain – there are countless situations that can occur in life that can affect you for a lifetime. You can either choose to let it consume you in a negative way, or let God help you to refocus in a more positive way. We chose the latter. What will you choose?

There is a verse in Matthew that reads, "What will it benefit a man if he gains the whole world yet loses his life? Or what will a man give in exchange for his life?" (Matthew 16:26, HCSB). This verse in Scripture is spoken by Jesus to His disciples as He is talking about someone who chooses to follow Him. He encourages them that there is more to life than being self-seeking.

I have heard my pastor say that in all the funerals in which he has served, he has yet to see a U-Haul following the hearse. You may even be familiar with the phrase, "You can't take it with you." When our life ends, there is not one physical thing from this world that will go to Heaven with us. We will leave everything behind. My pastor would sometimes say, "You can't take it with you, but you can send it ahead." He meant by this that as we live our lives, the things for which we pray, the people that we lead to the Lord, every good thing that we do in His name – those all become things with eternal value. Those are the things in life which are truly significant.

When we face various life-changing trials, we often become focused on the things that really matter. Did you tell your children that you loved them? Did you forgive when someone wronged you? Did you let go of mistakes and move forward? Did you shine for Jesus as brightly as possible?

These questions are best answered before tragedy strikes, but often get asked as a result. But now, while you have the chance, take the time to make things right between you and the Lord. Then make things right between you and the people about whom you care most in the world. Eternity is a long time to be separated from someone you love, and it's best to make each moment that we have count for something lasting. Tell those that you love that you love them. Make certain that they, too, have a relationship with the Lord. That they *know* Him, not just know *of* Him.

Setting priorities in our lives with an eye on an eternal impact is critical. Our families are our number one priority, second only to a relationship with God. What good does it really do to gain *stuff* in this life and lose your family or lose out on an eternity with the Lord? When we focus on the things that really matter, it takes a lot of pressure off the day-to-day. It makes it easier to "not sweat the small stuff." This had certainly been one of the impacts of our journey. While there were certainly things we needed to accomplish - including school - it just didn't carry the importance that it once had. There were more important things on which to focus and bigger dreams to fulfill.

Eternity is a long time to be separated from those you love. Make each moment count. Tell people you love them. Make certain that you and those you love <u>*know*</u> *the Lord, not just know of Him.*

God's Goodness in Giving Dreams

On one of our hospital stays, Keith and Caleb were talking about how much God had been doing for our family. God's goodness is always a wonderful thing on which to meditate! Caleb began to share with his dad about a concern that he had. He is typically fairly reserved on sharing his thoughts and feelings about things. Like me, he prefers to be a little more private. He told his dad that he was concerned about the numbness that was on his leg from where the surgeon had removed what was left of the tumor.

The incision was quite a long one, beginning above his knee and continuing past his ankle. After the incision itself had healed, he had a lot of fun with the scar. When children would gawk at the ugly scar, he would just look at them seriously and say, "Shark bite. Better stay out of the water, kids." Then he'd just laugh seeing their eyes widen. If they hung around long enough, he'd tell them his story about how God had miraculously healed him.

His concern this day, however, was not something he was laughing about. At the time of the operation, the surgeon had told us that it was unlikely that Caleb would be able to lift his foot at all. God had showed out big time, however, miraculously revealing paths for the surgeon's knife to travel to remove the tumor sliver without cutting a single nerve or artery that could have ended in amputation.

Caleb had kept his foot and astoundingly had even been able to lift it immediately after the surgery, though that had been deemed an impossibility. The surgeon told us following the surgery that the numbness he felt on the outside of his leg would likely last for months or even years because of the trauma to the nerves during the surgery. For the surgeon that was such a minor thing considering the 99.9% probability of cutting the nerve that would have been life changing for our son.

But it bothered Caleb that there was something about his leg that was not feeling right. And this wasn't coming from a place of ungratefulness for what God had already done. He just knew that if God had done that one important thing, why couldn't He do this little thing?

Keith told Caleb that God had promised us that if He began a good work in our lives, He would carry it to completion. Philippians 1:6 reads, "And I am convinced and sure of this very thing, that He Who began a good work in you will continue until the day of Jesus Christ [right up to the time of His return], developing [that good work] and perfecting and bringing it to full completion in you" (Amp). God is intentional. When He brings Scripture to your mind, it is purposeful - to bring hope, increase faith, or bring about some change. In fact, 2 Timothy 3:16-17 states, "All Scripture is inspired by God and is profitable for teaching, for rebuking, for correcting, for training in righteousness, so that the man of God may be complete, equipped for every good work" (HCSB).

Knowing that Scripture from Philippians stirred Keith. He knew that lingering numbness was not completeness, so he reached over and grabbed Caleb's leg to pray. Before the word "Father" passed his lips, he felt the presence of God move into the hospital room and a surge of power moved through his hands.

As he began to pray, Caleb said that the feeling in that part of his leg returned! Keith hadn't even gotten to the part in his prayer where he was going to quote Philippians 1:6 nor had he even said, "in Jesus' name" before the healing occurred. Just talking about the Scripture before they prayed stirred up their faith to believe the Word. There are so many stories in the Bible where Jesus tells people that their faith has made them well. This one was one that we got to live out.

God is intentional. When He brings Scripture to your mind, it is purposeful – to bring hope, increase faith, or bring about some change.

Our pastor came by the hospital to visit that day. Caleb could hardly wait to tell him what had happened. Pastor rejoiced and thanked God for meeting every need – spiritual, physical, and financial! We had a mountain of bills that we'd accrued because of the medicines and care Caleb had received, but strangely I was not worried.

I was thankful that the hospital was gracious enough to take care of Caleb despite what we owed and his care was never halted nor was anyone anything other than kind as they took care of us. All I could see when I looked at my reality was that my son was healed. Nothing else really mattered. I knew the hospital would work with us until they had been paid everything that was owed. More importantly, I knew that just as God had worked a miracle in healing my son, He was just as capable of working miracles for us financially. He had already shown so much favor, so we might as well keep dreaming big! Nothing was too difficult for God!

The Miraculous

It is an incredible thing to be able to see miracles, and we had already seen many. This did not make us special. We aren't any more special to God than anyone else! He loves

ALL His children, and desires to fill our lives with good things. Remember what ALL means? ALL means ALL!

The Bible is clear that God is not a respecter of persons. Acts chapter 10 tells a story about how a man named Cornelius had a Heavenly encounter during a time of prayer and fasting that led him to invite Peter (one of Jesus's disciples) to his home. In those days, it was not common for Jews and Gentiles to associate with one another. But when Cornelius told Peter about what he had seen, Peter said, "Now I really understand that God doesn't show favoritism, but in every nation the person who fears Him and does righteousness is acceptable to Him" (Acts 10:34-35, HCSB). Peter then shared the message of Jesus with the Gentiles and while he was speaking, Scripture says that "the Holy Spirit came down on all those who heard the message" (Acts 10:44, HCSB).

What an astounding revelation that had to have been for Peter and his fellow believers, that God was a God for ALL people, not just a select few. And what He does for one, He can do for another. He doesn't play favorites with His children, and you have a right to see provision for every need in your life in the same way that we did, and even greater! God can make a way where it seems impossible. We have seen it. We have lived it! We are not perfect people, but perfectly loved by a perfect God.

Be encouraged that you can trust Him and believe His Word! He is not mad at us for where we have failed or come short, He's mad about us. He has saved our son from death, and healed him completely and miraculously. Even the doctors were amazed! He has provided for our needs time and time again, and what He has done for us, He will do for you, too, because He loves you. And God is not finished with us yet. There are still areas in our lives where we have need. Caleb is missing a length of bone in his leg, and we are believing for God to regrow it! God has already shown that He can do the impossible, so why not dream big?

We are not perfect people,
but perfectly loved by a perfect God.

10

Powerful Words

Pleasant words are like a honeycomb,
sweet and delightful to the soul and healing to the body.
Proverbs 16:25 (AMP)

During our journey, Keith wrote a blog. Every few days or weeks, he would update our friends and family members on what was going on in our lives. When the Lord told me that I was to write this book, I cried out to Him, "But God! How can I remember the details of what happened? I know the main stories, but I love details. I don't want to make a mistake and mess up on the details of what happened."

It was then that God spoke to me and reminded me that Keith had written a blog detailing most of the events as they happened - all the ups and downs, the struggles, the pains, the victories, and the miracles! Every entry was dated. God spoke to my heart, saying, "This book is one of the purposes for which I had Keith write each day." Wow!!!

I knew that the blog was an outlet for Keith. At the time, it was hard for me to have him be so transparent about so many details of our private lives. But as I began to see how many people were reading and responding to him about his writing, and knowing that it gave people details that enabled them to pray with specificity, I felt at peace with the sharing.

Never in my wildest imaginings, however, did I anticipate reading over the blog and studying the details to restate it in story form five years later. But God sees far into our future and sets us up now for future successes so that no trial or difficulty is ever wasted. That is a thought of which I have often reminded myself when going through any life experience that is uncomfortable – that perhaps at its conclusion I would be able to share how God saw me through the difficulty with someone who might be facing something similar.

God sees far into our future
and sets us up now for future successes
so that no trial or difficulty is ever wasted.

God Doesn't Waste a Thing

God is not wasteful. In Scripture, there is a story of exponential blessing. Many people refer to this story as the story of the loaves and fish. You may already be very familiar with this story which is found in the book of John.

While Scripture doesn't say anything about a mother in this story, it does say that the boy had a lunch with him of five barley loaves and two fish. I suppose he might have had someone other than his mom who prepared the lunch for him.

He also could have caught his own fish, cooked them and made his own bread. You could actually put any person in the place of "the mom" in my imagination and my point would still be appropriate. But for the sake of my imagination here (and because it doesn't have any influence on the miracle Jesus performed) follow my line of thinking for a moment.

I can imagine that the mom of the little boy in the story got up early and packed the small lunch for her son as she set him off for the day. I can imagine that she placed it in a pouch that she had made to keep it from getting dirty as he went about his day. I can also imagine that she was satisfied that the lunch would be provision for him to satiate his hunger and give him the energy that he needed as he played or worked that day. I doubt that she had any idea that her labor and provision for one would have far-reaching effects. But God always desires to use the gifts He has placed in our hands to bring Him glory and produce wonderful results! We just have to be listening for His call and ready to respond with a resounding, "Yes!"

Scripture tells us that because of all the miraculous signs that Jesus performed, and His healing of the sick, a crowd followed Him wherever He went. People will come to a fire, y'all! At the beginning of this story, in the book of John, Jesus was sitting on a hill. He was surrounded by His disciples, and saw a huge crowd coming. John 6:5b states, "Turning to Philip, He (Jesus) asked, 'Where can we buy bread to feed all these people?'" (NLT).

Now Jesus knows everything. Scripture even tells us that Jesus knew exactly what He was getting ready to do, but was testing Philip. It was as though Jesus wanted Philip to be aware that there was a problem coming that was so big that it was impossible for him to solve even with the help of his friends. Philip responded that even if they all worked for months, they would never be able to afford to buy enough bread for everyone who was coming up that hill to see Jesus (John 6:7, NLT).

I have a feeling that none of the bakeries in town, if there even were any, could have possibly supplied enough bread for such a large crowd of people had Jesus and the disciples been near one and had enough money to purchase it all. Scripture tells us that there were five thousand men in the crowd, and that didn't count the women and children who were present. But there is no problem too big that it is insurmountable for Jesus.

One of the disciples told Jesus that there was a little boy in the crowd that had bread and fish. He also pointed out that it couldn't make enough of a difference considering how many people were there. But Jesus can use what seems too insignificant to even count as a possible solution to become, not only immediate provision for today, but also sustenance for tomorrow. And that was certainly about to be the case here. I can almost imagine Jesus saying, "Now, y'all watch this!!!" as He rubbed His hands back and forth in anticipation of what He was about to do.

Jesus can use what seems too insignificant to count as a solution to become immediate provision for today and sustenance for tomorrow.

Scripture tells us that Jesus had the disciples to have everyone to sit down on the grass. He gave thanks for the bread and fish and began to distribute it to those who were seated. The Bible says, "And they ate as much as they wanted. After everyone was full, Jesus told His disciples, 'Now gather the leftovers, so that nothing is wasted.' So they picked up the pieces and filled twelve baskets with scraps left by the people who had eaten from the five barley loaves" (John 6:11-13, NLT). As a mom of two teenage boys, I can tell you that five loaves and two fish wouldn't fill just the two of them. I have a hard time imagining that it could fill one of them. Imagine that small amount filling that many people up and they even had leftovers! What a miracle that was!

The crowd was already familiar with Jesus doing amazing things, so when they were told to sit down on the grass, I imagine they were both obedient and expectant. Can you imagine living life consistently obedient and expectant for miracles because you had been a personal witness to so many? I can imagine how awesome that would be!

The Lesson

The little bit that mama had packed for her son that morning (assuming that was who prepared the lunch) became the seed sown to produce a miraculous harvest that day. It also served to be a lesson the following day to the disciples. They learned not to be so concerned with the natural things of life, but to focus on things of eternal value. So not only was Jesus careful not to waste anything in the natural, He also did not waste an opportunity to help those closest to Him understand an important concept. He knew how limited His time was. Our time on earth is also limited. What a relief, what joy to know that there is nothing we walk through in life that is wasted. Every storm we endure, every trial we overcome can become a witness to God's power and provision that brings hope to those in the midst of a personal gale.

Positivity

As the months and weeks of treatment dwindled to days, it almost seemed unreal that we were finishing this part of our lives. We kept hearing words like "survivor" spoken about Caleb. What a powerful word to hear used from the lips of those who had earlier spoken of the possibility of death. The truth was that he was a survivor – we all were. We had endured a very difficult journey that most children do not have to even think about. And we had known several children who hadn't had the same outcome.

But more impressive than being a survivor was that he was healed. Not everyone will face cancer in their life time. Thank God for that! But most people will face things in their life for which they need healing. And being healed of God is a miraculous thing that is for *anyone* who is dealing with sickness on *any* level – physical, emotional, or spiritual.

Our future was filled with possibility. We had a few delays because of low counts, but the doctors said that was normal after receiving so many treatments. The final week of chemotherapy finally came. I had never been so excited to be in the hospital! That may seem like a peculiar attitude to have about a week-long hospital stay, but we were thrilled that it would be the very last one!

A dear friend recently wrote, "Often the only difference between our perception and reality is just our attitude" (PaulaAnnLambert, 2017). Having a good attitude about whatever situation you face certainly can impact your whole being and even influence your results! I have often heard, "attitude affects altitude." I'd rather have positive thoughts and feelings that line up with God's Word any day than feel symptoms of depression that so often accompany negative thoughts!

After Caleb's last week of treatment, we would only have to visit the clinic once a week. Following a month of that schedule, we would only have to go once a month to check his counts and flush the port. Six months after chemo, if everything still looked good, we could have the port removed, and would then only have to go back once every three months for scans and tests.

Temptation

Positive thoughts don't always come easily. We don't live in a bubble, and the enemy is always looking for opportunities to tempt us, to bring discouragement, or incite fear. It was even that way for Jesus. The gospels of Matthew, Mark, and Luke each tell us about a story often referred to as "the temptation of Christ."

Growing up in church, I'd heard this story many times. I knew that Jesus had fasted for forty days and that there were three specific temptations the enemy had used to test Jesus's understanding of who He was by tempting Him with satisfying fleshly hunger. He also tested who Jesus knew God to be by tempting Him with the promise of power and possessions (pride). Finally, He tested Jesus's understanding of God's power and authority even to the point of bringing to question God's love for Jesus and His promise to protect Jesus. Satan twisted Scripture to make it sound like it would be okay with God for Jesus to succumb to Satan's temptations.

With each temptation, however, Jesus modeled using the Word correctly to overcome the enemy. This brought victory in the end and is a powerful, true story that can change a life. Just that example alone is a great one on which to meditate. God made certain that we would have every tool necessary for overcoming the enemy. We are not powerless. Working the Word, speaking it over situations we face can be powerful.

God made certain that we would have every tool necessary at our disposal for overcoming the enemy. We are not powerless. The Word is powerful!

But that is not the end of the story. Something I missed until I was much older was the very last verse at the end of the story, and probably one that was omitted from my childhood Bible story books. It almost seemed like something you'd find in fine print, but it is quite clear in Scripture.

Luke 4:13 reads, "When the devil had finished tempting Jesus, he left Him until the next opportunity came" (NLT). The devil didn't just give up completely. Using Scripture certainly brings the win and causes the enemy to flee. James 4:7 states, "Submit yourselves therefore to God. Resist the devil, and he will flee from you" (KJV). I've already mentioned that verse in this book.

But just because the enemy flees doesn't mean that he isn't going to try again and again! 1 Peter 5:8 warns us, "Stay alert! Watch out for your great enemy, the devil. He prowls around like a roaring lion, looking for someone to devour" (NLT).

Lions don't just get hungry occasionally, either! According to the University of Minnesota's College of Biological Sciences, male lions can eat about 43 kg in a day (2015). That is close to one hundred pounds every single day! Therefore, Scripture tells us to be watchful. Jesus is the Son of God; and if the enemy tempted Him repeatedly and looked for other opportunities to tempt him, you can guarantee that we will have to fight him off more than once. Thankfully, God knew this and gave us the tools to do it, beginning with Scripture!

Attacks

With the final treatment upon us, we were rejoicing. Caleb had been through so many needle sticks in his port in the past year, that he no longer used the medicinal numbing cream when they were accessing it. It's amazing the painful things to which you can become accustomed. I had no idea what a blessing that port would be when the doctors put it in.

I remember being so concerned about them putting in the port before chemo started. I was confused about how it worked and the benefits of Caleb having one. At the beginning of this diagnosis we were rather completely at the mercy of the people who understood some of the obstacles that would lie ahead of us. It was uncharted territory for us and called for a lot of trust in people we didn't even know yet but would later come to deeply love and appreciate.

As the end of our journey loomed on the horizon, my mind began to wonder about what we would do when the port was removed. The port made accessing Caleb's blood vessels a cinch for the nurses. There was never any digging around trying to hit a vein when IV medication needed to be administered or blood work needed to be done. We had had that issue before. Once again, the enemy began to plague my mind with fear at a time when rejoicing should have been the only thought. But the enemy never wants to leave us alone, and like he did with Jesus, he is always looking for the next opportunity.

My thoughts rambled down the road of fear. Isn't it peculiar how letting your mind ramble tends to lend itself well for a hostile takeover? Perhaps that is why using self-control (one of the fruits of the Spirit – reference Galatians 5:22-23) is so important and why Scripture commands in 2 Corinthians 10:5 to take every thought captive. Your thoughts can lead you astray if you let them ramble.

Proverbs 3:5-6 speaks to the importance of our thought life as well. It is a commonly known verse and one many parents and teachers have children memorize early in their lives. I remember learning the King James version of Proverbs 3:5-6 on flashcard when I was learning how to properly write the letter "T." I was probably five years old. It is one of the Scriptures printed on my shower curtain, as well.

The Amplified Version, however, expounds on it so well. It reads, "Trust in and rely confidently on the Lord with all your heart and do not rely on your own insight or understanding. In all your ways know and acknowledge and recognize Him, and He will make your paths straight and smooth [removing obstacles that block your way]" (Proverbs 3:5-6, AMP).

We cannot rely on our own understanding. If we do, we may find ourselves going down a wayward path that leads to destruction. I have allowed that several times, taking bad news as fact or letting my mind think along the worst-case scenarios. That is neither helpful nor productive. And yet, that is exactly what I was allowing to happen, instead of controlling my thoughts and focusing on the Lord's ability.

Removing the chemo port seemed a very final thing in my mind. I began to be concerned that if the doctors removed the port, what would happen if the cancer came back? That was a thought I should have never ruminated on, and yet it came in many different forms. We had several people with whom we had become friends on our journey whose children had passed away. One child we knew had gotten a cancer-free diagnosis after undergoing treatment and then, at a post treatment scan, a new tumor was discovered. Not long after that, the child left this earthly home. I will never forget the day that the parent of that child asked me if I ever worried about the cancer returning.

Difficult Questions

Part of me wishes that I could have just lied and told them that I never thought about it; that I knew God would take care of Caleb, and we would never have to face this monster again. But first, it is a sin to lie. Second, I am a terrible liar – even when I am trying to conceal something in fun. My family and friends tell me that my face reads like a book. I can conceal secrets very well, but lie – that is a no for me. I don't even try, though at times I joke with my best friends that

I need to keep practicing. Honesty is the best policy anyway, right? But thirdly, how could I say that about my child when their child was no longer by their side? It almost didn't seem fair that my child was still with me. It was a tricky question to answer confidently without causing them pain.

Regardless, I chose honesty seasoned with love. 1 Corinthians 16:14 reads, "Let all that you do be done in love" (ESV). I explained that I did have that thought cross my mind from time-to-time. But just like in removing the port, I never let my mind travel a long way down that road. I would find a detour, with my map being God's Word.

That's practical advice for anyone needing redirection toward healthier, Scripturally sound mental direction. I can almost hear the words "recalculating, recalculating" like my GPS does when I have made a wrong turn. When you find your mind taking a detour down the wrong road, use God's Word as a map to recalculate where you need to be heading. I never even spent time considering the fact that the doctors would just reinstall a new port and we would go after it again. That was just too out-of-the-way for the direction I was heading.

When you find your mind taking a detour down the wrong road, use God's Word as a map to recalculate where you need to be heading.

Self-Control

Perhaps the reason my mind stopped so quickly was because I knew in my heart that this would just be allowing fear to reign. It does absolutely no good whatsoever to worry about what might happen in the future. I've often heard the expression that a ton of worry doesn't do an ounce of good. I have always liked that thought. If you can do something about a problem, then go after it. If there is nothing you can do to change a situation, then there is nothing to do other than pray.

Worry is pointless and unproductive, and it is immeasurably more silly to worry about something that you are not positive is coming to pass. I was attacked in my mind many times, but I never allowed my mind to stay there and I'd had a year of very intense training in keeping my thoughts captive. No matter what problem we faced, we would face it knowing that God was on our side and that He had provided every tool we would ever need to face anything that ever came our way – no matter the name.

It is sometimes hard to speak into the lives of people who have experienced great difficulties that you have not walked in yourself. I think that for me I feel that I have no right to tell them anything when I couldn't possibly understand the depth of their pain. If it is something like what I have faced, then I tend to feel a greater level of boldness.

Powerful Words of Life

While the Lord uses our negative experiences to speak life and hope to others, He also can use us to speak hope into situations where we have not walked, and our words are so powerful. Spending time in the Word and in prayer enables us to better know the character of God. It is when you can comprehend the character of God that you can compassionately counsel the confused and crestfallen with confidence, even if you have never walked in their shoes. It is a precious gift to be able to be light bearers and bring a powerfully encouraging word to someone.

When you can comprehend the character of God, you can compassionately counsel the confused and crestfallen with confidence.

We were given that opportunity many times. In the beginning, we modeled boldness for our children, speaking to people in the hospital and clinic. Keith was especially gifted with boldness, and ministered to several families who had received recent diagnoses. Through social media, I was able to learn about others who had a recent diagnosis and made a point to go visit them at the hospital when I happened to be there. I met some amazing people this way! Some of these people were in a boat like ours. But some had walked the journey, gotten clear scans and a good report, and had been diagnosed a second time.

I cannot even count the number of people who have sought out Keith or me to pray for healing for themselves or someone they love, especially after a cancer diagnosis. I find this to be such an honor, to be entrusted to believe for something with someone. It is also something that we take quite seriously - praying against those things using the powerful Word of God.

When Caleb began to have boldness in encouraging other children who, like him, were undergoing treatment, or when Joshua was able to encourage someone who was struggling, I was especially moved. Knowing that our words are powerful for yourself is one thing. To be able to give that power to someone else is special. And God did not call any of us to keep our stories of victories to ourselves. We are to bring light to the darkness. We must share God's goodness with those who don't know or who have forgotten.

Purpose

This is, in large part, why I believe the Lord asked me to write this book. It is my desire that some of the lessons that we learned on this journey will teach solid Biblical truths to the one who reads this manuscript and give them a good foundation on which to stand. I also hope that by sharing of some of the many wonderful miracles that happened to us, it will build the faith of the reader so that they may believe for miracles of their own.

God can take something the enemy meant for harm and turn it around. After that, He can even use it for His glorious purposes! Miracles of healing, provision, favor, abundance, and so much more are all within God's power. And the spectacular part is that He wants to do amazing things for us. There are many Scriptures that tell of remarkable miracles that happened before, during, and after Jesus walked this earth. And God is every bit as alive and active today as He was then.

God is the same no matter the second, minute, hour, or year of any struggle we face. I wonder if many are just not aware of the miracles God is performing on their behalf. Perhaps that is why some people believe that God doesn't do miracles any more. That simply isn't the case!

Scripture reads,

> "For God has said, 'I will never fail you. I will never abandon you.' So we can say with confidence, 'The Lord is my helper, so I will have no fear. What can mere people do to me?' Remember your leaders who taught you the word of God. Think of all the good that has come from their lives, and follow the example of their faith. Jesus Christ is the same yesterday, today, and forever. So do not be attracted by strange, new ideas. Your strength comes from God's grace." (Hebrews 13:5b-9a, NLT)

Miracles

Miracles are not strange, new ideas. They are recorded in the Bible, they are recorded in this book, and there are literally thousands of miracles you can find through legitimate Christian resources online and in other media formats as well. Miracles occur all around us, sometimes we just have to look for them! They aren't brand new at all, and if God will work these awesome miracles for my family, I know He will do it for you. What do you have the faith to believe God to do? Is there something that is impossible, something out of your realm of ability to perform? That sounds like a good starting point for God! There is absolutely nothing too difficult for God.

Luke 1:37 confirms that, "For nothing is impossible with God" (NLT). Matthew 19:26 reads, "But Jesus looked at them and said, 'With man this is impossible, but with God all things are possible" (ESV). In explaining to the disciples why they were unable to perform a particular miracle on their own, Jesus states in Matthew 17:20, "He said to them, 'Because of your little faith. For truly, I say to you, if you have faith like a grain of mustard seed, you will say to this mountain, move from here to there, and it will move and nothing will be impossible for you" (ESV). Mark 11:24 reads, "Therefore I say unto you, what things soever ye desire, when ye pray, believe that ye receive them, and ye shall have them" (KJV). Jeremiah 32:27 reads, "Behold, I am the Lord, the God of all flesh. Is there anything too hard for me?" (ESV).

There is nothing like digging into the Word of God and reading about the many miracles of Jesus and His disciples to build your faith! And the gospels and the book of Acts are a great place to start. Looking for what God is doing lately? It is all around us! There are so many testimonies of God's miraculous and divine provision available for us to read over or to listen to and increase in faith!

Review your own past and remind yourself of how God showed up or showed out! One of my favorite stories in the Bible is found in 1 Samuel chapter 30 in the town of Ziklag. (I think Ziklag is just fun to say!) But something terrible had happened there – one of the enemies of David had come into the town when the men were away at battle and had captured all of the women and children.

David's men were angry because their wives and children and other possessions had been taken, and were contemplating stoning him. But the second half of verse six reads, "But David encouraged himself in the Lord" (1 Samuel 30:6b, MEV). What powerful words! He asked the Lord if he should go after what had been theirs, and God responded that he should and that he would be successful. When David did what God agreed he should do, he was as victorious as God had told him he would be.

Sometimes you have people around you who will lift you up and encourage you. Having been the recipient of this many, many times, I can testify to how powerful those encouraging words are. But sometimes there are so many naysayers surrounding you that it feels like it could literally crush you under the weight of it all. I remember those times, too.

I remember one time in particular toward the beginning of our journey, one lady began to tell me how she knew someone who had been diagnosed with cancer and she began to inform me of how terrible it had been. I remember that my best friend quickly rescued me from her presence and the influence of her words. Words, both positive and negative, are very powerful. I am so thankful that my friend had the boldness and wisdom to pull me away from that situation. In times when you are burdened by the words you hear, you might, like David, have to encourage yourself!

Seek God

God is always ready to be found by you, and He is ready to communicate with you. Talk to Him and listen to what He responds. He always wants what is best for you. I am confident that your end will be victorious when you are walking in what He has ordained, even if the victory doesn't look like you think it will look. You will find encouragement when you talk to Him.

There is an old gospel hymn that was written by Cleavant Derricks, titled "Just a Little Talk with Jesus." It has been recorded by many artists over the years. The lyrics admonish us to "Have a little talk with Jesus. Let us tell Him all about our troubles. He will hear our faintest cry, He will answer by and by . . . You will find a little talk with Jesus makes it right" (G., 2012).

These are encouraging lyrics to me, knowing that I can talk to Jesus at any time, that He is always listening to me and that there is nothing I need withhold from Him. I wonder if sometimes we think our thoughts, opinions, or concerns will offend God.

I can assure you that He has "heard it all!" I mean, He knows everything and has always been here, so there is nothing we could think, say, or do that would shock Him. Disappoint Him, yes, but not shock or surprise Him. And that is especially reassuring when you feel you have asked for prayer so many times that you wonder if people ever get tired of hearing your requests. But be encouraged! God always wants you to talk to Him, whether you have a need or not!

We went to the Lord often, over big and little needs, to worship Him, or just to listen to what He was saying. We were tired of the many delays of the last treatment. The journey was nearing completion, however, and we were so thankful that the end was nearly upon us.

The day that Caleb received his last dosage was a day I will not soon forget. The doctors came in with a huge poster and a blow-up plastic guitar and celebrated with us. They were so excited for us that the chemotherapy was over, and everyone was all smiles. The next week at clinic, the nurses and other staff celebrated again with can after can of silly string and much hoopla just across the hall from where Caleb had spent many days connected by plastic tubes to powerful medicines attached to metal IV poles. I could scarcely believe that the celebration was real and that it would be a couple of weeks before we'd need to be in the room for a checkup without getting chemo.

Two weeks later, Caleb had a final PET scan. We awaited the results. His energy was returning. While he still had no hair, he was enjoying eating strawberries and lettuce and many things of which he had felt quite deprived over the last year and a half.

I remember buying our first big box of strawberries from a friend who owns a local strawberry farm. Caleb held that box in his lap all the way home. He could hardly wait for me to wash them! Watching Caleb eye those strawberries and get his first bite of his favorite fruit was heartwarming.

His test results from the scans came back and he received a diagnosis of "all clear." He didn't have to undergo radiation. Hearing that there is not a single bit of cancer is cause for much rejoicing. "Cancer free." Those are powerful words.

Dreams Fulfilled

We received a phone call a few weeks later from the Make A Wish Foundation in November. After a year of working on Caleb's wishes, they were able to make his top wish a reality. One very frosty evening, we waited in the empty parking lot across from the little post office and the flashing yellow light in our rural town, eagerly watching for any signs of movement coming down the barren road.

Caleb's desire had been for something that the whole family could enjoy. We saw a big box truck coming down the road, and when they opened the back and rolled out the four-seater motorized vehicle covered with balloons, Caleb was beside himself. As we watched his excitement, our minds darted back in time to a little boy silently crying about leg pain in the back seat on the way to church.

We remembered the hair-covered hand darting out of the shower curtain with a cry of alarm, the many days of sickness and weakness, painful muscle-burning shots, and blood transfusions. We thought about the wondering questions about why this had happened to him and what had he ever done to deserve any of this, the little boy sitting there biting his lip and squeezing my two fingers getting ready for yet another injection, and so many other traumatic memories. We saw our son, who had looked at those mountains and said to them to be cast into the sea – and we watched with him as the mountains had moved.

Keith told him that he wished Caleb wasn't getting a wish at all. It wasn't because he didn't want Caleb to have it, but because it came at such a high personal cost. If he'd never been sick, he'd never have gotten the wish. But God took something that the devil meant for his utter destruction and made something beautiful of it in His time.

Caleb understood. He'd lived through trauma after trauma. When he took the keys to the motorized vehicle, and inserted them into the ignition, it was like a new level of maturity encompassed him. Keith rubbed Caleb's peach-fuzz covered head, and we watched him drive off toward our home into the sunset.

Respect the Lord your God and serve Him.
Be loyal to Him. Make your promises in His name.
You should praise Him. He is your God.
He has done great and wonderful things for you.
You have seen them with your own eyes.
Deuteronomy 10:20-21 (ICB)

11

My Way Right Away

Now all glory to God, who is able,
through His mighty power at work within us,
to accomplish infinitely more than we might ask or think.
Ephesians 3:20 (NLT)

We live in a time of near instantaneousness. When we have an impressive thought, we can promptly share it on social media with the understanding that potentially millions of people can read and agree or disagree with our thoughts. While we may not want everything in life to be immediate for us, the things I pray for are usually things in which I want to see results right away. Who doesn't love that?

We know God hears us when we pray. 1 John 5:14-15 declares, "This is the confidence that we have in Him, that if we ask anything according to His will, He hears us. So, if we know that He hears whatever we ask, we know that we have whatever we asked of Him" (MEV). In fact, He knows our heart's desires better and even before we do.

There have been times when I have prayed over something and seen an immediate or nearly immediate answer.

I remember praying in the prayer room at church one Sunday morning and feeling impressed to go put my hands on the wrist of a woman in the room who was wearing a brace. She had a tremendous amount of pain in the wrist. As my husband and I prayed over her in the name of Jesus, she noticed significant improvement. We continued praying over her and she was able to remove the brace, move her wrist, and experienced no pain at all. Yay, God!

Quick Response

On another occasion, Keith was driving in the mountains by himself and praying. He felt the Lord leading him to make a music album. He is a tremendous musician, and hoped to put together an online fundraiser so that it could be accomplished.

He'd had this dream for years but had put it away on a shelf. He pulled that dream out, dusted it off, and wrote up a proposal of everything he was going to need. He began investing some money toward the project, putting his money where his heart was. Scripture reads, "For where your treasure is, there will your heart be also" (Matthew 6:21, KJV).

Months later, he was sharing from the platform at church about the blessing of the tither and giver. He shared how God had unexpectedly provided an extremely nice saxophone that he would need to do what God was calling him to do. He then made the statement that he was going to create an album! I was stunned.

I knew that he felt impressed that God wanted him to do it. God had told him that shortly after He told me to write this book, that they would go hand-in-hand. But to announce it from the pulpit on a Sunday morning?? Now he had no choice at all! He was going to have to follow through with what he said. I mean, the service was even streamed online! You know if it is on the internet, it MUST be true!

Well, life continued. A few weeks passed, and Keith went to work as always, in the little office building he had been using for years right beside our house. He felt he needed to get an office that was away from the house so that he could "go" to work and really be able to focus on his job. A new office would improve his access to the Internet as well, which was needed because of a new direction he was taking in his business.

We found an office space, rented it, and prepared to move in. On the day that we were moving his office furniture, I hurt my back trying to catch a heavy bookshelf that seemed to be falling. I was hardly able to do any kind of bending without a great deal of pain and even missed church that Sunday as a result. I watched the early service on my phone from my bed, with my legs and feet propped up on pillows to relieve the pressure on my back. During the worship time, I was having a conversation with the Lord. I was telling Him how great He was, singing along with the music from service, and just listening.

Hearing God

As I watched the service online, I could see my husband on the platform toward the back of the stage with his saxophone. He began to play while the soloist sang. It was a beautifully anointed song, and I was completely enjoying the moment when the Lord spoke to me that He was going to provide the funds for the album.

I continued my conversation with the Lord, just thanking Him for that. I told Him that I was excited about what He was telling me. I added that I was looking forward to hearing Keith tell me all about some major influx from his insurance business that would provide for the cost of the album. The Lord then clearly told me, "No. That is not how I am going to do it. I am going to provide for it completely. They are going to lay money on the altar (at church) and it will be enough."

I was flabbergasted at His announcement to me, but I told the Lord, "Okay!" I mean, what else should one say to the Lord? I continued watching the music service and heard nothing more from the Lord. I watched as the music ended, tithes and offerings were collected as usual, and the sermon started and finished. It was a great service. As there was nothing else much to do, I scrolled through social media on my phone for a while and rather lost track of time a bit.

A little after 11:00, I was scrolling through Facebook and noticed a live stream of the second service that was ongoing. My husband had his saxophone and was standing at the front of the platform in this service. My immediate thought was, “well that’s different!” I opened the stream to watch and hear what was going on.

One of the pastors was talking about our family and specifically about the album that Keith had felt impressed to produce. She went on to say that the Lord had told her that a sound would be coming out of this house and that this album would not only be a part of that but that it would be good ground for the congregation to sow into. She called for two offering buckets to be placed on the altar at the front of the podium and people began to place money into them for the album. I was absolutely stunned at what I was witnessing. It had happened in exact detail as the Lord had told me.

After the worship set, I received a very excited text from my husband asking me if I had been watching online. I enthusiastically told him about my interchange with the Lord earlier that morning and we were both in awe over what had happened. When the funds given for the project over two weeks were collected and compared to the amount Keith had written down on November 11th - over a year earlier - as the amount needed for the project, the difference was only $20. The Lord had provided it all without needing to put together a fundraiser or financing it on our own.

Waiting for Answers

If only every prayer I prayed gave me the results I longed for minutes after praying. But sometimes we pray for things and the wait is longer. Sometimes prayers are answered very slowly over time. Sometimes the results are not what we prayed for at all.

What do we do then? Do we quit? Do we get angry and throw blame around? Do we look for a justification of why the Lord didn't move the way we had asked or when we wanted it? This is an excruciating reality which we sometimes face. I confess that I have had all those emotions, at times, when things didn't go as I had prayed on our journey.

The doctors' reports sometimes permeated every fiber of my being, and those reports did not always line up with the promise for which I was believing. It was as though I could hear their words over and over in my head more than I could the Scripture on which I had been standing. It was in those times that I reached out to those closest to me. Those people in my closest circle were such a gift to me in times when I wasn't sure what to pray or when I felt I had prayed all that I knew to pray.

What to Pray When I Don't Know What to Pray

I was recently praying and believing for the miraculous for someone dear to me, but I wasn't seeing the results for which I was hoping. When I got to the point that I was feeling frustration because of the delayed answer, I again enlisted the advice of my closest circle of friends. One of my friends gently reminded me to keep praying the Word.

I listened to her advice and then took it to prayer. My conversation with God really came more from a place of frustration than faith, but as I became silent to hear what He had to say about my dilemma, I heard, "It isn't your job to do the healing. It's only your job to pray and believe My Word."

I think I had come to the place where I felt it was up to me. We had seen multiple victories in our walk. And while I knew that the miracles were evidence of the hand of God in our life – His goodness and provision, I had begun to feel that somehow it was my responsibility to make sure that the things for which I prayed happened, and quickly. It was my prayers, my reading Scripture aloud, my praise to our Healer, MY WORKS that made the Word work – and God lovingly reminded me that it wasn't my job at all.

It isn't your job to do the healing.
It's only your job to pray and believe My Word.

It isn't up to us to make things happen in prayer the way that we want. While faith moves God, we cannot manipulate Him to do our will. I continued to pray. I prayed Scripture aloud and silently. I had faith that His Word was infallible and I could trust Him no matter what I saw in the natural or what happened in physical reality.

The following Sunday, during worship, I felt the Spirit of the Lord remind me of the words He had communicated to me the previous week. It isn't my job to bring healing or any other miracle for which I am praying. It is only my job to pray His Word in faith. It is my job to believe Him and trust in Him. It doesn't matter what I think I know - God knows best. He is still God. He is still good. He still loves each of us. He is still able to do more than we can even imagine, and nothing is impossible for Him. I only had to believe.

Things don't always come about in the way we expect. This does not mean that the Word of God has failed, nor does it mean that you have been ineffective. The Word reads, in James 5:16b, "The earnest prayer of a righteous person has great power and produces wonderful results" (NLT). When what you have prayed for doesn't seem to happen the way that you thought it would, the enemy of our souls would have us believe the lie that we have failed in some way or that God Himself has failed us. But those are lies. It is not our job to work the miracle, only to believe in the God who is able to perform the miracle.

But when Jesus overheard what was said, He told the synagogue leader, "Don't be afraid. Only believe."
Mark 5:36 (HCSB)

Fighting the Good Fight of Faith

I recently read an article in which the author said, "The way you fight the devil is by opening your mouth and saying what God says" (Meyer, n.d.). How true is that! That is exactly what Jesus did, and that is exactly what we should do as well. God says our prayers are productive (James 5:16), so when we hear anything that is contrary to the Word of God, we know it is a lie from the enemy. Combat those lies with the Word of Truth, using your Sword of the Spirit, the Word of God. Therefore, it is critical that we spend time in the Word. The more we read or listen to Scripture, the more we will recognize a lie and have the resources to combat it.

I am thankful that when I have had wonderful seasons in life and when I have had difficult ones, I have always had a wonderful, Godly family and an equally wonderful church family to encircle me with their influence. There is a story in Exodus chapter 17, during the time when Moses was leading the children of Israel out of bondage and toward the promise land, when another army attacked them. Moses gave instructions to Joshua to go out and fight the opposing army on behalf of the Israelites, and that he would go stand at the top of the hill with his staff. Two helpers went with Moses. Exodus 17:11 reads, "As long as Moses held up the staff in his hand, the Israelites had the advantage. But whenever he dropped his hand, the Amalekites gained the advantage" (NLT).

Lift Your Hands

I used to participate in a puppet group. I was quite good at it, making the puppets really come to life. I even won several awards at competition. But after about a 7 to 10-minute puppet sketch, my arms would be worn out!

My favorite puppet had a head full of heavy brown yarn pulled into pigtails and legs that I could hold over my resting arm. My mama made her for me. That puppet is beautiful and I love her. She is also quite heavy, and seems to grow heavier the longer I hold her up. I can't even imagine having to hold my arms up much longer than a few minutes, especially if life or death was in the balance!

But Moses had two friends at his side. Scripture tells us that Moses began to get tired. His friends got a stone for him to sit on, and they stood on either side and held up his hands for him. The Bible says, "So his hands held steady until sunset. As a result, Joshua overwhelmed the army of Amalek in battle" (Exodus 17:12b-13, NLT). In this story, it was not only a matter of Moses's perseverance, but the steadfastness of his friends surrounding him that brought on the victory.

Friends

Another one of my favorite verses in the Bible is found in Proverbs, the book of wisdom. Verse seventeen of chapter twenty-seven reads, "Just as iron sharpens iron, friends sharpen the minds of each other" (CEV). It might be that your family stands beside you, helping you in the battles and successes of life. It might be your church family, praying and walking the journey beside you. It might be your closest circle of friends, your neighbors, your co-workers, or your small group who are the ones by your side. But I do know that whoever it is, we need one another. We need people who will hold us up, hold us accountable, and help us stay encouraged. We need people who will cry with us when we are hurt, get us up and back going again, speak words of life and hope to us, and help us celebrate life's victories. We were not made to be alone. We need one another.

It is these people who are with us when we aren't seeing immediate results about things for which we are praying. It is they who can shine the light on our darkest situations when our battery seems to have gone dim. These are the ones who will help us hold up our hands in a fight. If you don't have people like this in your life, please let me encourage you to find a good church, get involved, and find some of these people with whom to surround yourself. Friendship, in whatever form, is a gift from God. The Kingdom of God is all about family. He never intended us to be alone, and He certainly never intended for us to fight our battles alone.

Our family and friends saw us through the difficult days. The days when things weren't going our way. The prayers they lifted on our behalf were more valuable than anything else. Just knowing they were there, caring about us, texting us, visiting us – these things were priceless to us.

Share Your Story

I love that the story in Exodus doesn't just end with the Israelites winning the victory. It continues, stating, "After the victory, the Lord instructed Moses, 'Write this down on a scroll as a permanent reminder, and read it aloud to Joshua'" (Exodus 17:14a-b, NLT). The Lord was the one who wanted the events of the battle recorded so that the story would not be forgotten, but shared. Our stories, our testimonies, carry life and hope within them. They are meant to be shared to impact others, give them direction, inspire them to keep striving in the direction that God is taking them, and God gets the glory from all the victories we achieve together.

One of my best friends often says, "We are better together." She is absolutely correct. Even when promises seemed delayed, it is better when you have someone with you on the journey. There were doctors and nurses helping us along the way, encouraging us, praying with us, and giving us helpful instructions. No matter the ups and downs we faced, God's people were always by our sides.

A group of nurses from a local surgical center and a Sunday School class took up money and provided all the gifts for my boys for two Christmases. We had friends who gathered and led a worship fundraiser to help toward our hospital bills. Another church, one full of friends but which we had never attended, had a worship concert fundraiser that paid the final hospital bill! What a blessing our friends and family are to us. I couldn't imagine walking this path alone. Sharing your gifts, talents, finances, time – these things add up. Together, we can do more.

So, as I sit here today, I am watching my children write on their computers about what God taught them on this journey. I can hear my husband playing music for his new album, and I am overwhelmed by the goodness of God in my life. While we are not perfect and don't have every aspect of our lives all together, we are walking out our journey one step at the time. We are facing and climbing each mountain in our path and are confident that we will be victorious. Like the Psalmist David, we proclaim, "Yet I am confident I will see the Lord's goodness while I am here in the land of the living" (Psalm 27:13, NLT). God is so good.

Oh, how He loves us and wants the very best for us! How He wants us to include Him in every aspect of our day! How He longs to commune with us, see His promises attained in our lives, and our dreams fulfilled. He wants us to dream big, think outside of the box, and take Him at His Word. He wants us to stretch our faith and trust Him.

For what miracles are you believing? What promises in Scripture are you praying out loud and on what are you standing? He is the God of Miracles, and we can believe in Him. He worked so many miracles for us and He is more than able to meet every miraculous need in your life as well - even if you cannot see any way that it can ever happen. He loves you so much. Believe it.

God does wonderful things that cannot be understood.
He does so many miracles they cannot be counted.
Job 5:9 (ICB)

A Word from Keith

So shall My word be that goes forth from My mouth;
It shall not return to Me void,
But it shall accomplish what I please,
And it shall prosper in the thing for which I sent it.
Isaiah 55:11 (NKJV)

I remember one particular day in the spring of 1994 like it was yesterday. I was traveling full-time on the road with the Christian group, Truth. We were making our way back through the central United States after a tour on the West Coast. This particular day we were in Broken Arrow, OK.

When I auditioned for Truth the first time in 1992, it was while sitting on their bus after one of their concerts in our hometown of Augusta, GA. We were sitting in the parking lot of the LaQuinta Inn around midnight and I was playing my sax for their musical director, Joel Siegel, who is one of the most talented sax players I have ever known.

I actually got the call from Joel in the summer of 1993 that Truth wanted me to come on the road. I was to go to Mobile, AL, where Truth was headquartered to meet and audition for the director, Roger Breland. It was then that I found out that I was actually taking Joel's place in the group.

The other sax player in the group has recently gone home to be with the Lord. His name was Lanny Cox. Lanny and Joel both had a huge impact on me. When I went on the road in August of 1993, Joel stayed for the first two weeks I was there to make sure the transition was easy. He and his new bride, Amy, were heading to Tulsa to start school at Rhema Bible College under the leading of Kenneth Hagin.

A couple of days after the Siegels left for Bible college, Truth left for an Eastern European tour. I had learned more and more about the Holy Spirit over the last few years as I pressed in deeper to God and His Word. I was from a mainline denomination that did not believe in the baptism of the Holy Spirit with evidence of speaking in other tongues. But after reading many passages about it, including really feeling God speaking to me about it while reading Acts chapter 19, I knew there was more.

On our first night in Budapest, Hungary, I was sharing the room with Lanny Cox, who would become one of my closest friends. He had been sharing with me as I asked him questions about Holy Spirit. That night in Budapest, Lanny prayed for me and I received the baptism! A river of worship poured out of me and I began to speak in other tongues. I would learn much over the next few months about this new wonderful world of being led by the Spirit.

So, back to that day in the spring of 1994. Joel Siegel was living in the Broken Arrow area just outside of Tulsa and was there that day to see his friends in Truth. That afternoon while walking next to the Truth bus, Joel just appeared through some tall shrubbery and trees. He had a set of cassettes he said the Lord wanted me to have, so he bought it for me. It was a series of Kenneth Hagin's teachings that was titled, "Answered Prayer: An Attainable Goal."

A few days after this, I began listening to the teaching where he talked about finding what the Word of God says about whatever you are facing, and praying and speaking that Scripture over your life and situation. He taught me to pray the Word of God. It changed me deeply. I had never heard this level of faith being taught. Over the next few weeks, I listened to it over and over.

Fast forward to 2011. Holly and I were sitting at a conference table on the 4th floor of the Children's Hospital of Georgia. Two of the most amazing doctors had just walked out so we could have a few minutes to digest the horrible news they had just dropped in our laps - that our son had a rare form of cancer.

I told Holly that we had talked faith and lived faith to the best of our ability. We had applied the Word to our lives. We had a wonderful life in God. But I told her that this was where the rubber meets the road. We had to believe that God would do exactly what His Word says - that He would heal our son. We spoke it out. We read Scriptures aloud. We posted them all over the house on index cards so they would always be before our eyes. We were careful with what we said and what we saw. We put up guardrails to our eyes, ears, and tongue. This was life or death. Our faith HAD to work!

A Word from Keith

I remember when I first heard that it was Ewing's Sarcoma. I had never heard of it, so I made a big mistake - I went to Google to find out about it! I saw two articles that said the same thing - the 5 years' survival rate for this rare form of cancer was around 70% for children, if caught early.

I did what was a really bad thing for a computer in those days. I wanted that stuff gone from in front of my eyes, so instead of shutting down the computer, I reached over and yanked the plug from the wall. I immediately began quoting Scriptures that promised long life and healing over our son. We continued that practice daily. God really built our faith during those days as we pressed in.

I really hope this book blesses you. One very important fact that we had to understand early on is that sickness and disease are not put on us to teach us something. God gave us His WORD to teach us. John 10:10 says that, "the thief comes to steal, kill, and destroy." That is not God's MO. Jesus said in that same verse that He came that we would have abundant life!

Did we learn a lot during that season? Absolutely! It was one of the biggest growth periods in our lives. But God did not put cancer on our son so that would happen. He took what the enemy meant for harm and destruction and used it for HIS glory! God desires mercy above judgement. Don't ever think that our good Father wants anything but abundant life for you. Get in His Word and get it in your heart; get it in your spirit. He's a good, good Father!

A Word from Caleb

The thief does not come, except to steal and kill and destroy. I came that they may have life, and that they may have it more abundantly.
John 10:10 (MEV)

Before I start getting into bigger detail, I want to establish the fact that there's always hope, even in the direst situations. Maybe your brother is going through cancer. Maybe you've recently had a miscarriage. Maybe even your mom, who you've been close to for your whole life, just died in a car accident that wasn't even her fault. Maybe you, your spouse, or a parent has lost a job and you don't know what you will do next. Whatever the case may be, God is always good. He's not turned on and off with a button, and He doesn't give out on you. I understand that many things can damage your faith sometimes, but like I said, there's always hope.

I'd like to expand on this, so I'll give you a bit of my story BEHIND my story. Everyone who has read this book has heard of the awesome miracles God performed in my life. You know that we had been scared, but prayed through it. But no one ever heard the gruesome side of it – the side that I never told anyone.

Let's start with 2011, 5 years ago. (Wow, it's been a long time, I just realized). The day I found out about the rash, which went from my ankle to the back of my knee. It didn't last long, but it was in a perfectly straight line. It went away after a few days, but a few days after that is when things started to get scary.

I recall sitting on the couch with my family watching Robert Morris preach on TV. My leg had already been hurting a little bit, but now it had progressed to a more severe pain. I remember sitting there, on that couch, the pain quickly becoming more unbearable.

I'd like to just say I don't cry unless it's something that either physically or emotionally hurts to the extreme - so I practically NEVER cry. Well, this time, I started to cry. I don't know if the source of the pain was the tumor pushing against my bone, if it was swelling that was just now starting to really hurt, or what it was exactly. I just knew that something was seriously wrong, and I didn't know what.

I had been getting short pains in my body like growing pains, as I was just starting to hit my growth spurt. For a little while, I had assumed the sharp pain in my left leg below the knee was just a super growing pain, but I had started to worry that it was more than that. I wasn't familiar with cancer or tumors. I even thought that chemo was spelled "Kemo."

Skip ahead to Sunday morning a couple of weeks later, on the way to church. I woke up, all drowsy, the pain still slightly there. At this point, I had gotten pretty scared of this pain. Maybe it was a bit more than I had anticipated.

We got in the car to take the nearly-hour-long drive to church. About 10 minutes out, the pain started to come back stronger than before. This was torturing my mind, and I told myself I would be acting like a baby if I were to complain to Mom or Dad about the pain. I tried to suck it up and be a man at 11 years old, but it was no use.

I began to cry, trying to be quiet in the backseat so I wouldn't be a bother. I wanted to cut off my leg. I wanted this pain gone – whatever it took. I didn't understand it, and I felt hopeless. Dad looked up in the center mirror and saw me crying silently, holding my leg and trembling like a leaf in pain and fear. He asked me what was wrong, and I hesitantly told him that my leg was hurting again.

I could see the deep concern in his eyes as he focused on the road again. There was small talk between Mom and Dad. Then Mom told me that Dad was going to drive to church (as he was the band director there) and mom would drive me to the hospital to try to find out what was wrong.

I remember walking into the hospital ER, my heart racing as I walked past the waiting patients. A few of them looked up at me as I walked with Mom to the desk. The last time we had gone to the ER was when I had the rash. They had looked at it and told us not to worry about it. They had said that the pain was nothing but growing pains.

This time they did a CT scan, and I wanted to cry during the whole scan. I was nearly controlled by fear. They did many scans that day, and the doctors concluded that we needed a biopsy the next day. After the surgery, the surgeon came out and told my parents that the growth in my leg had a neoplastic trace to it, which meant, I probably had cancer. Sure enough, in October, the results came back from the Mayo Clinic, and it was Ewing's Sarcoma with a tumor the size of a billiard ball.

Now, my Mom could have NEVER told me I had cancer. She would have broken down in tears before she could even get the sentence out. But I remember the day my Dad broke the news to me in the parking garage of the hospital, on the third floor in a corner spot. We were sitting in his old gray Chevy Suburban.

I remember my stomach being so knotted up I could hardly breathe, before he even told me. He looked at me directly in the eyes, and I could see the pain and tears in his eyes as he opened his mouth. "The doctors found that . . . it is cancer."

My heart seemingly stopped. Immediately, I found myself not breathing, not blinking - my vision blurring as I began to soak this in. I felt hopeless, thinking for sure that I would not survive this. At 11 years old, being told that you have a terminal illness and hearing from others that you could possibly die is calamitous and haunting.

I asked Dad if I was going to die. Dad explained that there was a 7 out of 10 survival rate but that in God's eyes, I have a 10/10 survival rate and there's no possible chance that I could die. Right then, I didn't want to hear that. I didn't want this. Nobody does. I wanted to be at home with not a care in the world.

None of my friends had cancer, I was the odd one out! Why was this happening to me? Why couldn't it be somebody across the world that had just gotten away with a heinous crime? Why couldn't it be someone who deserved cancer?

All this had gone through my head in a matter of seconds. Sadness and anger crept over me, and I started to cry. I feared for my life. I wanted to grow up and have a family. I wanted to eventually have a house in the mountains and a fast car. I wanted my own dog, and most importantly, I wanted to be with my friends and family for the rest of my life. And I didn't want that to be a short time.

I was overwhelmed about the whole thing. The first few weeks was overwhelming. I was overwhelmed after my port insertion, after I started to lose my hair, and after I had gone pale due to low white blood cell counts. I was overwhelmed about having to vomit numerous times a day, even on an empty stomach when the only thing I could vomit out was stomach acid which burned and stung my throat.

I had started to believe that I deserved this somehow. Almost every night I'd wake up crying - silently *begging* God for forgiveness. I would plead with Him that I didn't know what I had done, but that I was sorry. I would tell Him that if He would tell me what I did, it would never happen again.

I played Dad's words over, and over, and over again. "*It is cancer.*" It played in my head for the longest time. I had begun to have thoughts that God wasn't healing me because this was my punishment for something.

A few weeks later, we moved in with my grandmother. It was better on gas not to drive an hour every day in a V8 powered, all-wheel drive SUV that weighed more than 5,000 pounds and got about 10 miles to the gallon. In November, the Bay of the Holy Spirit Revival came to my church. I got healed completely, and God killed the tumor and every last cell relating to it. I felt like a free person, like I had conquered the world.

Christmas came. I got a crossbow and a nice TV along with some smaller things like die cast cars and candy (lots of candy). It was the first time since the Bay of the Holy Spirit Revival that I had been truly joyous. We had food. We told jokes. We laughed together, and we spent beloved time with *family.* I think that from that point on, I started to lighten up a good bit. I was learning that God was on my side, that He was with me all the time. I learned that I hadn't done anything to deserve this, and that God hadn't made me sick. He doesn't put sickness on anybody to teach them a lesson or punish them for something they've done. I learned that while bad things sometimes happen to good people, God would turn the whole thing around for my good.

All I had to do now was finish chemo. No sweat, right? Wrong. Later on, I found out that on Christmas morning, my cousin Raul had passed away. He was young, not much older than me. He'd had cancer. Shortly before that, my friend Davey, who I'd met at the hospital's clinic, passed away. Another good friend of mine named Chad passed away. Then my friend Ri'anna, who'd survived cancer, had to have her left leg amputated above the ankle. After that happened, my buddy Jason was re-diagnosed with cancer after being free of it for months. These were all people close to my age I'd come to know at the hospital who, like me, were battling cancer. After all this, two of my Mom's friends got cancer. One of them, who had been in her wedding, passed away. I was seeing so much of it – and it seemed to be happening all on top of each other, one after another, while I was facing cancer myself.

These events were very discouraging, but even though they made me feel sad I wasn't letting stuff keep me down. I was sure that I would survive this thing. I believe Satan wanted to remind me of these deaths and hurts to get me discouraged. He knew because of what I was saying that I was starting to feel encouraged and less scared, and I was telling people that God healed me. Those people all had a special place in my heart. Nevertheless, I had to keep my spirits up.

I remember my big surgery in February when the surgeon basically told me that I would never be able to lift my left foot again. They said that they would have to cut a nerve wrapped around the tumor. They also said that there were arteries in my leg that they would likely cut. If they had to cut one or two, it would be okay. If they cut three, however, they would have to cut off my leg.

I don't think I was ever really bothered by the fact that I might lose a leg. I didn't think my leg was overly important for having just for the sake of having a leg. What I was shattered about was the fact that I wouldn't be able to drive my four-wheeler, and that was my favorite thing to do. During the surgery God worked a miracle and not only did the surgeon not cut any nerves or blood vessels, but I could move my foot immediately after surgery! There would be nothing stopping me from riding my four-wheeler at all (except for my parents making me do my school work).

The night I finished chemo, when the IV machine alarm went off indicating that the bag of chemo had run out, I looked at my Mom in excitement. "Am I done??" My face brightened.

"Yep, that's it." She replied.

I could see the thousand-pound burden being lifted off her shoulders as she said that. A few weeks later, my hair began to grow back. I was no longer sick (the best part of being cancer free), and my life was finally normal after what seemed like the longest time. I was cancer-free, my white blood cell count was higher than ever, and *I felt so liberated.*

There had been so many rules - lists of things I couldn't do while I was undergoing treatment, and many of those rules had been lifted. There were still some things I couldn't do even after chemotherapy was over and I had recovered. I had to be mindful that I only had one bone in my lower leg instead of the two I had before. But I could eat strawberries again (my favorite), I could touch things without having to use hand sanitizer every five minutes. I could even hold my dog close again.

In conclusion, I'd like to just tell you this. If God can heal me of cancer through many mighty miracles, He can heal you of neck pain. He can heal you of a headache. Shoot, He can heal you of scoliosis. I've seen it happen! God is not a God of lack or disappointment. He is a God of provision and compassion. He is a healer. With God, nothing is impossible. He loves you and wants only the best for you. He is not a God of mini miracles; He is a God of many miracles. Believe it!

A Word from Joshua

Carefully obey the commands I am giving you today.
Love the Lord your God.
Serve Him with your whole being.
Deuteronomy 11:13 (ICB)

Hey, I'm Josh. The verse I chose as my favorite, Deuteronomy 11:13, talks about loving, obeying, and serving God. It is a verse that holds a promise of provision. The Bible says in the next verse that if you will do these things, God will take care of sending what you need your way at the right time. If you are going through something tough, just obey God. He loves you and wants only good things for you.

When I was 9 years old, my brother had cancer. People sometimes joke about cancer because they don't understand exactly how terrible it is. But cancer is not something to joke about. Life isn't a joke. I tend to get upset when people joke about things like that. But God is a healer. That's no joke, either. Sometimes people overlook that when dealing with an illness.

When Caleb was 11 and I was 9, he started getting a lot of pain in his legs. Many people told him it was just growing pains, but it was more than that. One Sunday we were heading to church and the pain was extremely bad that morning, so my mom took him to the hospital. I remember I was in my Sunday School class, and my dad came in and told me we had to go. So he and I went rushing to Mom in their friend's car, since Mom had our car.

We hurried down to the hospital to learn that Caleb had a growth on his leg. They were saying it might be a tumor. Being 9 years old, I didn't understand what any of that was. When I found out, I was trying my best to distract myself, but nothing was working. I remember having to go to the clinic every day, and it was the worst place to be. I remember having to spend the night at the hospital so often. It was such a horrible place to be, because you could never sleep. It was uncomfortable, and you were always bored. It was just a bad experience all around.

People often came to visit, though. That made me feel better even though we were going through some hard things. My advice to someone going through something difficult is to try not to think about how tough things seem to be. Instead, focus on God and the good things that are coming ahead. Look for the good things God is doing around you then, too.

Our church held a revival, and that's the night that Caleb got healed. It relieved so much pressure off us. I could finally relax. I thank God that He healed Caleb and kept my family together.

The biggest thing that I learned as a result of our journey is that anything is possible through God – not to let fear control you. When you're going through stuff, sometimes that's a fact that people overlook. I believe that since we were walking by faith, Caleb got healed. We often looked at Caleb, laid hands on him, and said, "You are healed in Jesus name." If you are someone who is going through sickness or something bad like that, never lose hope. There are verses in the Bible that promise us healing and we can speak those verses over ourselves or people we care about. Proverbs 18:21 reads, “Death and life are in the power of the tongue, and those who love it will eat its fruits.” To me, that means that our words have meaning. They matter. They are powerful.

After Caleb got healed, he had chemo for a little while longer. Not long after that, our walk through cancer was over. I thank God for everything He did on our journey. I learned a lot about how He provides for us and how much people cared about us. I also learned how to tell other people about how good God is and how much He loves them. Even in the bad stuff, there was good stuff to learn because God is always good.

Scripture List

On our journey, we had Scripture written out on index cards and posted everywhere so that we could frequently see and read the verses on which we were standing for Caleb's healing. I have placed all the Scripture references from this book onto the following pages so that you could refer to them during your personal prayer time as you believe God for miracles in your own life! We are believing for a miracle with you!

Exodus 15:26 He said, "If you diligently listen to the voice of the LORD your God, and do what is right in His sight, and give ear to His commandments, and keep all His statutes, I will not afflict you with any of the diseases with which I have afflicted the Egyptians. For I am the LORD who heals you." (MEV)

Exodus 17:11 As long as Moses held up the staff in his hand, the Israelites had the advantage. But whenever he dropped his hand, the Amalekites gained the advantage. (NLT)

Exodus 17:12b-13 So his hands held steady until sunset. As a result, Joshua overwhelmed the army of Amalek in battle. (NLT)

Exodus 17:14a-b "After the victory, the Lord instructed Moses, 'Write this down on a scroll as a permanent reminder, and read it aloud to Joshua." (NLT)

Deuteronomy 10:20-21 Respect the Lord your God and serve Him. Be loyal to Him. Make your promises in His name. You should praise Him. He is your God. He has done great and wonderful things for you. You have seen them with your own eyes. (ICB)

Deuteronomy 11:13 Carefully obey the commands I am giving you today. Love the Lord your God. Serve Him with your whole being. (ICB)

Deuteronomy 31:6 Be strong and of a good courage. Fear not, nor be afraid of them, for the Lord your God, it is He who goes with you. He will not fail you, nor forsake you. (MEV)

1 Samuel 17:47 And everyone assembled here will know that the Lord rescues His people, but not with sword and spear. This is the Lord's battle, and He will give you to us! (NLT)

Job 5:9 God does wonderful things that cannot be understood. He does so many miracles they cannot be counted. (ICB)

Psalm 27:13 Yet I am confident I will see the Lord's goodness while I am here in the land of the living. (NLT)

Psalm 37:23 The steps of a good man are ordered by the Lord: and he delighteth in His way. (KJV)

Psalm 84:11 For the Lord God is a sun and shield; the Lord bestows grace and favor and honor; no good thing will He withhold from those who walk uprightly. (AMP)

Psalm 91:10 No harm will come to you; no plague will come near your tent. (HCSB)

Psalm 91:16 With long life I will satisfy him, and show him My salvation. (NKJV)

Psalm 103: 2-5 Bless the LORD, O my soul, and forget not all His benefits, who forgives all your iniquities, who heals all your diseases, who redeems your life from the pit, who crowns you with lovingkindness and tender mercies, who satisfies your mouth with good things, so that your youth is renewed like the eagle's. (MEV)

Psalm 107:1 Give thanks to the Lord, for He is good; His faithful love endures forever. (MEV)

Psalm 118:17 I shall not die, but I shall live and declare the works of the LORD. (MEV)

Psalm 141:2 Set a guard, O Lord, over my mouth; keep watch over the door of my lips! (ESV)

Proverbs 3:5-6 Trust in and rely confidently on the Lord with all your heart and do not rely on your own insight or understanding. In all your ways know and acknowledge and recognize Him, and He will make your paths straight and smooth [removing obstacles that block your way]. (AMP)

Proverbs 3:24 When you lie down, you will not be afraid; Yes, you will lie down and your sleep will be sweet. (MEV)

Proverbs 12:18 There is one whose rash words are like sword thrusts, but the tongue of the wise brings healing. (ESV)

Proverbs 13:12 Hope deferred makes the heart sick, but a dream fulfilled is a tree of life. (NLT)

Proverbs 16:25 Pleasant words are like a honeycomb, sweet and delightful to the soul and healing to the body. (AMP)

Proverbs 27:17 Just as iron sharpens iron, friends sharpen the minds of each other. (CEV)

Proverbs 18:7 A fool's mouth is his destruction, and his lips are the snare of his soul. (MEV)

Proverbs 18:21 Death and life are in the power of the tongue, and those who love it will eat its fruit. (MEV)

Proverbs 20:18 Plans succeed through good counsel; don't go to war without wise advice. (NLT)

Ecclesiastes 3:11 God has also given us a desire to know the future. God certainly does everything at just the right time. But we can never completely understand what He is doing. (ICB)

Ecclesiastes 4:9-12 Two people are better off than one, for they can help each other succeed. If one person falls, the other can reach out and help. But someone who falls alone is in real trouble. Likewise, two people lying close together can keep each other warm. But how can one be warm alone? A person standing alone can be attacked and defeated, but two can stand back-to-back and conquer. Three are even better, for a triple-braided cord is not easily broken. (NLT)

Ecclesiastes 7:8 The end of a matter is better than its beginning; a patient spirit is better than a proud spirit. (HCSB)

Isaiah 4:5b-6 There will be a covering over every person. This covering will be a place of safety. It will protect the people from the heat of the sun. It will be a safe place to hide from the storm and rain. (ICB)

Isaiah 40:31 But those who wait for the Lord [who expect, look for, and hope in Him] will gain new strength *and* renew their power; They will lift up their wings [and rise up close to God] like eagles [rising toward the sun]; They will run and not become weary, they will walk and not grow tired. (AMP)

Isaiah 53:4-5 Yet it was our weaknesses He carried; it was our sorrows (sicknesses) that weighed him down. And we thought His troubles were a punishment from God, a punishment for His own sins! But He was pierced for our rebellion, crushed for our sins. He was beaten so we could be whole. He was whipped so we could be healed. (NLT)

Isaiah 54:13 All your sons shall be taught of the LORD, and great shall be the peace of your sons. (MEV)

Isaiah 55:11 So shall My word be that goes forth from My mouth; it shall not return to Me void, but it shall accomplish that which I please, and it shall prosper in the thing for which I sent it. (MEV)

Isaiah 61:2b-3 To comfort all who mourn, to preserve those who mourn in Zion, to give them beauty for ashes, the oil of joy for mourning, the garment of praise for the spirit of heaviness, that they might be called trees of righteousness, the planting of the Lord, that He might be glorified. (MEV)

Jeremiah 1:12 Then the Lord said to me, "You have seen well. For I will hasten My word to perform it." (MEV)

Jeremiah 1:12 The Lord said to me, "You have seen correctly, for I am watching to see that My word is fulfilled." (NIV)

Jeremiah 29:11 "For I know the plans I have for you," declares the Lord, "plans to prosper you and not to harm you, plans to give you hope and a future." (NIV)

Jeremiah 32:27 I am the Lord. I am the God of every person on the earth. You know that nothing is impossible for me. (NLT)

Zephaniah 3:17 The Lord your God is in your midst, the mighty One will save. He will rejoice over you with gladness, He will quiet you with His love, He will rejoice over you with singing. (NKJV)

Matthew 5:15 In the same way, let your good deeds shine out for all to see, so that everyone will praise your Heavenly Father. (NLT)

Matthew 6:21 For where your treasure is, there will your heart be also. (KJV)

Matthew 12:36 I tell you, on the day of judgment people will give account for every careless word they speak. (ESV)

Matthew 16:26 What will it benefit a man if he gains the whole world yet loses his life? Or what will a man give in exchange for his life? (HCSB)

Matthew 17:20b "I tell you the truth. If your faith is as big as a mustard seed, you can say to this mountain, 'Move from here to there.' And the mountain will move. All things will be possible for you." (ICB)

Matthew 18:10 "Beware that you don't look down on any of these little ones (children). For I tell you that in Heaven, their angels are always in the presence of my heavenly Father." (NLT)

Mark 5:36 But when Jesus overheard what was said, he told the synagogue leader, "Don't be afraid. Only believe." (HCSB)

Luke 4:13 When the devil had finished tempting Jesus, he left Him until the next opportunity came. (NLT)

Luke 8:25 "Where is your faith?" (MEV)

Luke 11:9 "And so I tell you, keep on asking, and you will receive what you ask for. Keep on seeking, and you will find. Keep on knocking, and the door will be open to you." (NLT)

John 3:16 For God so [greatly] loved and dearly prized the world, that He[even] gave His [One and] only begotten Son, so that whoever believes and trusts in Him [as Savior] shall not perish, but have eternal life. (AMP)

John 6:63 It is not the flesh that gives a person life. It is the spirit that gives life. The words I told you are spirit, and so they give life. (ICB)

John 10:10 The thief comes only to steal and kill and destroy; I came that they may have life, and have *it* abundantly. (NASB)

John 16:33 These things I have spoken to you, that in Me you may have peace. In the world you will have tribulation; but be of good cheer, I have overcome the world. (NKJV)

Acts 10:34-35 "Now I really understand that God doesn't show favoritism, but in every nation the person who fears Him and does righteousness is acceptable to Him." (HCSB)

Romans 8:31 What shall we say about such wonderful things as these? If God is for us, who can ever be against us? (NLT)

Romans 10:9 If you confess with your mouth the Lord Jesus and believe in your heart that God has raised Him from the dead, you will be saved. (NKJV)

Romans 12:3 For I say, through the grace given unto me, to every man that is among you, not to think of himself more highly than he ought to think, but to think soberly, according as God hath dealt to every man the measure of faith. (KJV)

Romans 15:13 Now may the God of hope fill you with all joy and peace in believing, so that you may abound in hope, through the power of the Holy Spirit. (MEV)

Romans 15:15 "Nevertheless, brothers, I have written even more boldly to you on some points, to remind you, because of the grace that is given to me from God." (MEV)

1 Corinthians 2:14 But the natural man does not receive the things of the Spirit of God, for they are foolishness to him; nor can he know them, because they are spiritually discerned. (MEV)

1 Corinthians 16:14 Let all that you do be done in love. (ESV)

2 Corinthians 1:20-22 Whatever God has promised gets stamped with the Yes of Jesus. In Him, this is what we preach and pray, the great Amen, God's Yes and our Yes together, gloriously evident. God affirms us, making us a sure thing in Christ, putting His Yes within us. By His Spirit He has stamped us with His eternal pledge - a sure beginning of what He is destined to complete. (MSG)

2 Corinthians 5:7 For we walk by faith, not by sight. (MEV)

2 Corinthians 10:3 For though we walk in the flesh, we do not war according to the flesh. (NKJV)

2 Corinthians 10: 4 For the weapons of our warfare are not carnal, but mighty through God to the pulling down of strongholds. (MEV)

2 Corinthians 10:5 Casting down imaginations and every high thing that exalts itself against the knowledge of God, bringing every thought into captivity to the obedience of Christ. (MEV)

2 Corinthians 12:9 But He said to me, "My grace is sufficient for you, for My strength is made perfect in weakness." Therefore, most gladly I will boast in my weaknesses, that the power of Christ may rest upon me. (MEV)

Galatians 3:13 Christ has redeemed us from the curse of the law by being made a curse for us—as it is written, "Cursed is everyone who hangs on a tree." (MEV)

Galatians 5:22-23 But the fruit of the Spirit is love, joy, peace, patience, gentleness, goodness, faith, meekness, and self-control; against such there is no law. (MEV)

Galatians 6:2 Bear one another's burdens, and so fulfill the law of Christ. (ESV)

Ephesians 2:8-9 For by grace you have been saved through faith, and that not of yourselves, it is the gift of God, not of works, lest anyone should boast. (NKJV)

Ephesians 2:10 For we are God's masterpiece. He has created us anew in Christ Jesus, so we can do the good things He planned for us long ago. (NLT)

Ephesians 3:20 Now all glory to God, who is able, through His might power at work within us, to accomplish infinitely more than we might ask or think. (NLT)

Ephesians 3:20-21 God can do anything; you know – far more than you could ever imagine or guess or request in your wildest dreams! He does it not by pushing us around but by working within us, His Spirit deeply and gently within us. (MSG)

Ephesians 4:29 Let no corrupting talk come out of your mouths, but only such as is good for building up, as fits the occasion, that it may give grace to those who hear. (ESV)

Ephesians 6:2-3 "Honor your father and mother," which is the first commandment with a promise, "so that it may be well with you and you may live long on the earth." (MEV)

Philippians 1:6 And I am convinced and sure of this very thing, that He Who began a good work in you will continue until the day of Jesus Christ [right up to the time of His return], developing [that good work] and perfecting and bringing it to full completion in you. (AMP)

Philippians 4:8 And now, dear brothers and sisters, one final thing. Fix your thoughts on what is true, and honorable, and right, and pure, and lovely, and admirable. Think about things that are excellent and worthy of praise. (NLT)

Philippians 4:19 And this same God who takes care of me will supply all your needs from His glorious riches, which have been given to us in Christ Jesus. (NLT)

Philippians 4:19 And my God will supply every need of yours according to His riches in Christ Jesus. (ESV)

1 Thessalonians 2:13 Therefore, we never stop thanking God that when you received His message from us, you didn't think of our words as mere human ideas. You accepted what we said as the very Word of God – which, of course, it is. And this Word continues to work in you who believe. (NLT)

1 Thessalonians 5:16-18 Always be joyful. Never stop praying. Be thankful in all circumstances, for this is God's will for you who belong to Christ Jesus. (NLT)

2 Timothy 3:16-17 All Scripture is inspired by God and is profitable for teaching, for rebuking, for correcting, for training in righteousness, so that the man of God may be complete, equipped for every good work. (HCSB)

Titus 2:11-15 For the grace of God that brings salvation has appeared to all men, teaching us that, denying ungodliness and worldly desires, we should live soberly, righteously, and in godliness in this present world, as we await the blessed hope and the appearing of the glory of our great God and Savior Jesus Christ, who gave Himself for us, that He might redeem us from all lawlessness and purify for Himself a special people, zealous of good works. Teach these things, exhort, and rebuke with all authority. Let no one despise you. (MEV)

Hebrews 1:14 Are not all the angels ministering spirits sent out [by God] to serve (accompany, protect) those who will inherit salvation? [Of course they are!] (AMP)

Hebrews 6:19a This hope is a strong and trustworthy anchor for our souls. (NLT)

Hebrews 11:1 Faith is the confidence that what we hope for will actually happen; it gives us assurance about things we cannot see. (NLT)

Hebrews 11:6 Now without faith it is impossible to please God, for the one who draws near to Him must believe that He exists and rewards those who seek Him. (HCSB)

Hebrews 13:5b-6a For God has said, "I will never fail you. I will never abandon you." So we can say with confidence, "The Lord is my helper, so I will have no fear." (NLT)

Hebrews 13:8 Jesus Christ is the same yesterday, and today, and forever. (MEV)

Hebrews 13:15 "Through Him, therefore, let us at all times offer up to God a sacrifice of praise, which is the fruit of lips that thankfully acknowledge *and* confess *and* glorify His name." (AMP)

James 4:7 Resist the devil and he will flee from you. (NKJV)

James 4:8 Draw near to God, and He will draw near to you. Cleanse your hands, you sinners, and purify your hearts, you double-minded. (MEV)

James 5:16b The earnest prayer of a righteous person has great power and produces wonderful results. (NLT)

1 Peter 2:24 He Himself bore our sins in His own body on the tree that we, being dead to sins, should live unto righteousness. "By His wounds you were healed." (MEV)

1 Peter 5:8 Stay alert! Watch out for your great enemy, the devil. He prowls around like a roaring lion, looking for someone to devour. (NLT)

1 John 5:14-15 This is the confidence that we have in Him, that if we ask anything according to His will, He hears us. So if we know that He hears whatever we ask, we know that we have whatever we asked of Him. (MEV)

Revelation 12:11 They defeated him through the blood of the Lamb and the bold word of their witness. (MSG)

References

Bay Revival. (2016). *Wikipedia.* Retrieved February 8, 2017, from https://en.wikipedia.org/wiki/Bay_Revival

Brewer, C. (1995). Music and Learning: Integrating Music in the Classroom. *John Hopkins University.* Retrieved October 27, 2015, from http://education.jhu.edu/PD/newhorizons/strategies/topics/Arts in Education/brewer.htm

College of Biological Sciences. (2015). Retrieved June 15, 2017, from https://cbs.umn.edu/research/labs/lionresearch/faq

Derrer, D. (Ed.). (2014). Ewing's Sarcoma: Causes, Prognosis, Stages, Symptoms, and Treatments. *WebMD.* Retrieved October 27, 2015, from http://www.webmd.com/cancer/ewings-sarcoma

Encourage. (n.d.). *Dictionary.com Unabridged.* Retrieved October 27, 2015, from http://dictionary.reference.com/browse/encourage

Ephron, N. (Director). (1998). *You've Got Mail* [Motion Picture]. [With Tom Hanks, Meg Ryan, & Greg Kinnear]. United States: Warner Brothers.

G. (2012). Rev Cleavant Derrick Sings his Composition, Just a Little Talk with Jesus.wmv. Retrieved August 3, 2017, from https://www.youtube.com/watch?v=br-qMVfJhLw

Hayford, J. (2015). The Sacrifice of Praise. *Jack Hayford Ministries.* Retrieved October 28, 2015, from http://www.jackhayford.org/teaching/devotional/the-sacrifice-of-praise/

Hayford, J. (2015). Prayer - Part 2. *Jack Hayford Ministries.* Retrieved November 10, 2015, from http://www.jackhayford.org/teaching/devotional/prayer-part-2/

Hillsong Live. (2011). *It Is Well With My Soul* [CD Single]. Australia: Hillsong Music Australia.

Johnson, B. (2015). Mission Possible. *God TV.* Retrieved November 9, 2015, from http://god.tv/mission-possible/video/mission-possible/day-5-morning-session-bill-johnson

Johnson, B. (2017). The Way of Faith. *YouTube.* Retrieved August 1, 2017, from https:/www.youtube.com/watch?v=fXFNWZ4Zg1o. Posted on YouTube by J.J. Martin from Bethel TV

Low White Blood Cell Count (Neutropenia). (n.d.). *Children's Oncology Group.* Retrieved February 8, 2017, from https://www.childrensoncologygroup.org/index.php/lowwhitebloodcellcount

Meyer, J. (n.d.). How to Defeat Your Doubts and Feed Your Faith. Retrieved July 31, 2017, from https://www.joycemeyer.org/articles/ea.aspx?article=how_to_defeat_your_doubts

Miller, S. (2013). True & Apparent Wind. *School of Sailing*. Retrieved November 9, 2015, from http://www.schoolofsailing.net/true-and-apparent-wind.html

Milligan, I. (2012). The Ultimate Gide to Understanding the Dreams You Dream. Shippensburg, PA: Destiny Image Publishers, Inc.

Miracle. (n.d). Merriam-Webster. Retrieved February 9, 2017, from https://www.merriamwebster.com/dictionary/miracle

Pagana, K. (PhD, RN). (2009). What Does the Absolute Neutrophil Count Tell You. *American Nurse Today*. Retrieved February 8, 2017, from https://www.americannursetoday.com/what-does-the-absolute-neutrophil-count-tell-you/

PaulaAnnLambert. (2017, June 1). Often the only difference between our perception and reality is just our attitude. [Tweet]. https://twitter.com/PaulaAnnLambert/status/870264040873918465

Proof is in the Pudding. (2014). *Grammarist*. Retrieved February 9, 2017, at http://grammarist.com/usage/proof-is-in-the-pudding/

Rhema. (2014). *Bible Study Tools*. Retrieved November 10, 2015, from http://www.biblestudytools.com/lexicons/greek/kjv/rhema.html

Sacrifice. (n.d.). *Dictionary.com Unabridged.* Retrieved October 28, 2015, from http://dictionary.reference.com/browse/sacrifice?s=t

Sacrifice. (n.d.). *Blue Letter Bible.* Retrieved October 28, 2015, from http://www.blueletterbible.orghttps://www.blueletterbible.org/search/Dictionary/viewTopic.cfm

Chapman S. (1988). *Real Life Conversations* [CD]. Brentwood, TN: Sparrow Records.

Supernatural. (2015). *Merriam-Webster.* Retrieved November 5, 2015, from http://www.merriam-webster.com/dictionary/supernatural

Thompson, A. (2014). How Do Dust Devils Form. *Scientific American.* Retrieved October 24, 2015, from http://www.scientificamerican.com/article/how-do-dust-devils-form

Before You Go

Thank you for purchasing and reading *Believing for a Miracle*. I appreciate your support and I hope that you found it to be encouraging! This book is available in print and eBook versions from Amazon. If you liked what you read, please take a moment and rate this book online and share your recommendation of this book with others! Your good opinions shared with others are my best advertisements! Thank you!

Holly Murray

Stay up to date with the Murray family. You can access Holly's website at hollydmurray.com for photos from their journey, her blog, to request prayer, and other valuable and encouraging information. Connect via Facebook with the author by searching for @hollydmurrayauthor and liking the page. Follow on Twitter by searching for @hollydmurray. She would love hearing from you!

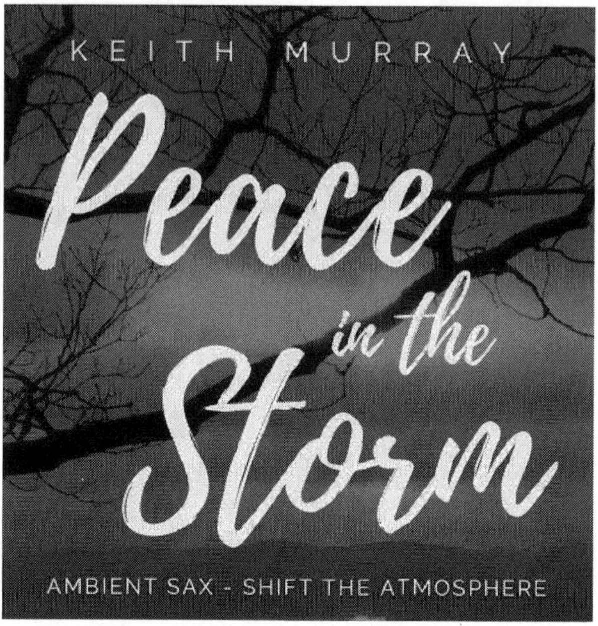

Keith Murray combines his skills as a musician and worshipper with an understanding of the tones and pitches of music and its effect on the body in his new album, *Peace in the Storm*. Feel peace wash over you as you listen to his original music at various healing frequencies. Ideal for times of rest, Bible study and meditation, or just to bring a relaxing shift to the atmosphere around you.

Get more information about ordering this mood-changing album from his Facebook page, Ambient Sax – Shifting the Atmosphere, by searching for @ambientsax. You can also get updates from his website at ambientsax.com.

ORDER YOUR COPY TODAY!

Miracles for which I am Believing

Made in the USA
Columbia, SC
10 March 2022

57132352R00150